MW00880301

UP FROM
HANGING DOG

(WHEN YOU'RE BORN IN HANGING DOG,
THE ONLY WAY TO GO IS UP!)

RAY B. ROGERS

Edited by
BRADFORD ROGERS

worldsongs

CONTENTS

This book is dedicated to two very important people in my life: My wife Lucy and my son Bradford.

Lucy encouraged me to keep on writing when I was questioning if it was really worth the effort.
She read my writings and made significant suggestions for improvement.

Bradford put my stories online so my extended family could learn of their roots and not forget our heritage.

Although I was encouraged to publish a book, I would never have done so if Bradford had not taken the bull by the horns and "got 'er done."

Bradford and Lucy's efforts to make me a writer and author remind me of the spirit that brought me "Up From Hanging Dog."

Connect at
RayBRogers.com

First Edition–2019
Copyright ©2019 Worldsongs, Inc.

ISBN 9781092510462

Worldsongs Media
4062 Peachtree Rd. NE #A-313
Brookhaven, GA 30319

U.S. trade bookstores and wholesalers:
Please contact Worldsongs Books at bradford.rogers@WorldsongsInc.com

PREFACE

UP FROM HANGING DOG

When I tell people I was born in a three-room shack without indoor plumbing in a little corner of western North Carolina called Hanging Dog, they must think I've led a miserable life. But that's not true.

I didn't know we were poor. We were surrounded by people that had even less than our family. Our poor neighbors up Hall Top Road didn't have a large garden with fresh vegetables, and they didn't have chickens and ducks and fresh eggs. They didn't fatten a hog or two to supply ham and sausage for breakfast. They didn't enjoy fresh milk and home-churned butter, like we got from our two cows, Buttercup and Ole Horney.

We didn't talk about being poor, but by today's standards we were. We didn't know how lucky we were that the Lord had supplied us with healthy organic food. But we didn't forget to thank him.

Dad "returned thanks" at almost every meal, and he remembered to acknowledge "those who prepared it." Mostly mom, with some help from us kids.

Dad once asked the youngest of our brood to say the blessing. Sister Dale was about three or four years old. She had been taught a proper blessing, but the cheerleaders at a recent football game had really impressed her.

Her blessing went like this:

> *Big dog, little dog,*
> *flop-eared pup...*
> *Come on Waynesville,*
> *eat 'em up!*

My friend Sheldon wrote in one of his books that I was born in a cabin. When I said I was born in a shack, he told me that "cabin" sounded better. But that wasn't Hanging Dog, where shacks prevailed.

In fact, these shacks were my Grandfather Medford's retirement plan. He rented them for ten dollars a month. I've said that when you are born in a three-room shack on Hanging Dog, the only way to go is up. I didn't know my school teacher father would light in me a burning desire to go to college.

I watched my father set an example as he went from a teaching job at nineteen, making thirty-five dollars a month, to eventually become president of the North Carolina Education Association.

My mother didn't get to finish her schooling since her mother Maggie died young. Mom had to raise her younger siblings in addition to her own family of six children. She always regretted not having a better education, and I felt her pain.

I've always been very independent. Seeing unemployment and poverty up close during the Great Depression, I wanted to insure that I would never be in a dependent position.

I decided that I must further my education. I would go "up from Hanging Dog."

-*Ray B. Rogers*

PART I

GROWING UP IN HANGING DOG

1

STREAKING THROUGH HANGING DOG

THE SETTING for this tawdry little tale was Hanging Dog, North Carolina. I wrote about Hanging Dog in my first book, *Depression Baby*. My brother Mark says that Hanging Dog is not only a place, but a state of mind. The keen insight of my brother is accurate and right on target, and I graciously accept his words of wisdom.

Streaking was a phenomenon of the 1970s, I believe. It occurred on College campuses and in shopping centers across these United States. There was even a song written about this mostly outdoor sport, practiced by both naked men and women.

The Streak, written by Ray Stephens in 1974, injected a lot of fun into our society and became a hit. Maybe streaking started with a dare: *I dare you to run, naked as a jaybird, from the dorm to the student center and back*. Or maybe someone lost a bet and had to pay off by taking a naked sprint.

It seems that Hanging Dog may have been an early leader or maybe even originated streaking. Historians will have to sort this out.

This event occurred in 1932 when I was about three years old, and my father, Frank Rogers, told me the story. Frankly speaking (as we said in our family), my Dad was always very accurate in his storytelling, missing few details.

We lived in a little three room house with no indoor plumbing. Dad had to heat water on the wood stove in the kitchen and pour it into a galvanized tub to prepare for my bath. Even though I had made it known that I did not want a bath, Dad picked me up and placed me in the tub.

Apparently, the tendency to strongly express myself came to me early. I hopped out of the tub, ran over to the fireplace, grabbed the poker and proceeded to rub soot on my body.

Dad attempted to place me in the tub again, but I ran out of the house stark naked, two or three doors down the road toward the little corner grocery store. Dad, in his wisdom, decided to let this play out, and just followed me to the store.

I knew the store owner, so I told him that my Dad was being mean to me and that I wanted him to call the law. People who lived in these parts did not call the police or the sheriff, they called "the law."

There was a scruffy-looking old man with a full beard in the store. He was not a pretty sight, to say the least. He came over to me.

"Sonny," he said, "if your Dad isn't treating you right, you can just come home with me."

I took one look at him and decided, right then and there, that maybe Dad wasn't so bad after all.

Dad and I walked peacefully back to the house and I am sure that it took a lot of soap to wash off all of that soot.

Well, maybe this was not streaking in its purest form. But just remember, streaking started on Hanging Dog, and will always be its claim to fame.

2

THE SCHOOL BULLY

IT WAS my first day at my new school, Waynesville Township Junior High School. The Rogers family had moved back from Jupiter to our house at Hanging Dog.

I was just walking down the hallway alone and minding my own business when someone came up behind me and grabbed my right arm and jerked me toward the open door of a classroom.

"Come in here," he ordered.

I pulled away and said "No, I'm going down the hall."

He tried to pull me into the classroom again, and we proceeded to have a fight right then and there. The teachers broke up the fight fairly quickly, with no serious consequences.

Little did I know that the school's number one bully had hit on me that first day of school. I wondered why I wasn't chastised by the teachers or called out in any way. The teachers had to have known who started the altercation, for they had probably encountered similar problems before.

Little did I know how lucky I was to have been hit on before I knew of the bully's reputation, for I might have been intimidated by his demeanor. Little did I know that by standing up to him and by fighting back, I'd guaranteed that he'd never bother me again. Later on, I learned that he had bullied a friend of mine all through grammar school.

In the eleventh grade, we both played on the varsity basketball team. He was the one who would elbow his own teammates in practice games, but he never elbowed me, for he knew he would not have an easy time of it.

At that time, it seems that bullying was a boy/man thing. However, today it appears to be a different scenario. Teenage girls make newspaper headlines by bullying on the internet, causing one poor victim to commit suicide. A sad but true event.

Humans are not the only species that endure this anomaly. Where did the term "henpecked" originate, other than in the barnyard? And every farm boy knows which is the top cow in the herd and which cow is cowed by all of the others. (Pun intended.)

Sometimes, I wondered how the bully was so fortunate as to marry one of the prettiest girls in our school. Then I learned that some girls are just attracted to the bad boys. Maybe I should have been badder—ha!

The thing about clichés is that they're usually true. What goes around comes around, and at the end of the day, one gets what he deserves.

You see, the bully died suddenly of a heart attack in his early thirties.

THE GAMES PEOPLE PLAY

(LITTLE PEOPLE, THAT IS...)

RED ROVER, Red Rover, let Johnny come over! How often is this echoed today across the playgrounds of America? Not a lot, I would venture to say.

Many of you have never heard of this playground game, where two sides are chosen and each side lines up facing each other. Each line holds hands and one side calls a name from the other side with a challenge for that person—let's say, Johnny—to run between any two individuals in their line and cause them to break their clasped hands. Of course, Johnny would have to run with some speed and force to break the other line.

When I grew up in the thirties and the forties, games like red rover and dodge ball which involved a lot of physical activity were common.

If there was a pile of dirt found anywhere, this initiated a game of king of the mountain, where one kid would climb to the top of the mound and establish himself (or sometimes herself) as King.

The object of the game would be to take the King off the

mountain by any means short of throwing things, and establish a new King. This game would make mothers wonder how in the world little Johnny could get so dirty—but it was good, clean fun for kids of this era.

Recess with physical games became great stress-breakers for students who needed to get away from the books for a little while. In fact, I never heard stress even discussed at that time, because life was usually lived in a manner that did not create stress.

Today, I read of school administrators who have eliminated recess from their schools curriculum. I'm sure that there are current school boards who cringe at the prospect that these physical games would create lawsuits by the score—with some justification. There were schoolyard accidents then, a few scrapes and bruises, but it wasn't any big deal. It was just a part of growing up.

Childhood obesity in Western North Carolina in the thirties was almost unknown. Children played tag or hide and seek when they came home from school, and they may have chased "lightning bugs" (Yankees called them fireflies) until bedtime.

They also had chores to do after school. But there were also quieter, less active, games to play. Marbles was one of these, and it was always easy to find some bare ground to draw a circle on and place some marbles in the circle.

Little boys had their favorite shooter or taw with which they shot the "mibs" (marbles within the ring) out of the ring. Sometimes steel bearings were used as shooters, but they would often break the glass marbles and were sometimes outlawed. Marbles were sometimes played for keeps and the best marble players would accumulate a lot of marbles.

Playing for keeps was frowned upon by some parents, and having a large cloth bag of marbles, always with a drawstring on top, might place one in jeopardy. Incidentally, these cloth marble bags originally held tobacco and most dads were smokers. This was before the Surgeon General condemned smoking.

Little girls had their own games such as jumping rope and some became very skillful. It was fun to watch them and listen to the chants they sang as they played this game. Also, girls (mostly) played hopscotch and it was common to see hopscotch patterns scratched in the clay playgrounds or on sidewalks in town.

Both boys and girls played jacks. When my wife Lucy was a little girl, she owned a pet raccoon who liked to watch her play jacks. He would watch her intently for a while, and then he would take his little paw and grab some jacks and run away. He had a secret hiding place for his loot.

When Lucy finally located the hiding place in the attic, she found some of her jacks and also some beads, a ring and other shiny objects. Lucy was given the orphan raccoon when it was a baby and she raised it on a bottle. It was the best pet she ever had with her pet fox running a close second.

In the mountains we didn't have to wait for snow to do some sliding. We would find a steep hill or bank with a lot of pine straw or broom sedge on it and then all we needed was a large piece of cardboard and a-sliding we would go.

Mountain boys would make a game of almost anything. A metal rim could be pushed along and controlled by a properly configured piece of heavy wire. Barefoot boys with imagination drove those wheels at race track speeds.

Boys in the country were never bored. If we found a water snake sunning himself on a rock near a creek, we would gather some rocks and slip up on the snake and turn loose a barrage of stones. The same strategy was used when we located a hornet's nest, except one had to be prepared to run like a rabbit to keep from getting stung if a rock hit the hornet's nest.

Boys Scouts used to play tug-of-war and teenagers used to

play spin-the-bottle and school children used to play red rover, and you know what? I just wonder if the video games played today are really more fun than the games people used to play?

4

A VISIT TO THE OLD HOME PLACE

WE TURNED off the road that follows Crabtree Creek to its head-waters, into a lane now called Duckett Drive which led to the house where grandfather John Francis Rogers and grandmother Mary Elizabeth lived. A little creek ran beside the lane fed by springs farther up the valley.

We immediately saw the large white frame farmhouse standing majestically on a little knoll surrounded by a picket fence. I didn't know at the time that this home was built by ancestors from my mother's side of the family in about 1895. Great-uncle "Big" Charlie Medford, great-uncle Taylor and great-grandfather Eldridge Medford brought their saws and hammers and their buildings skills from Iron Duff to construct what has become a part of our heritage over a hundred years later.

Tillie ran out to greet us, wagging her tail with the happiness of the moment. Tillie, a shepherd mix cow dog, would become my constant companion for the summer. She would be by my side as I carried water to the fields to quench the thirst of my grandfather, my three uncles, Herschel, Jack and John, and a hired hand.

Every 10-year-old boy needs a buddy and Tillie filled the bill. There was a cornstalk I kept laying beside the back porch and she would grab one end and I would grab the other and we would play tug of war as we ran barefoot toward the barn. The same ritual was repeated as we returned to the house. Tillie followed us up the fieldstone walk, up the steps, and onto the open porch.

As I opened the front door, there was a stairway to my left that led to the bedrooms. The entire house had walls of beaded wood that us mountain folks often called ceiling. Only my grandparents slept on the first floor.

To my right was the parlor. You don't hear about parlors much anymore. We have living rooms, great rooms and dens, even man caves today, but no parlors.

A parlor was mostly for the womenfolk. There was a piano in grandmother's parlor. (But her spinning wheel was not there, contrary to my recollection in the story "There's an old Spinning Wheel in the Parlor," in *Depression Baby*. The spinning wheel sat on a landing near the staircase.)

The parlor must be ready for company at all times. No clutter there! A neighbor or relative, or even the preacher, might just drop by at any time. Drop-ins were common then. There were no phones to check to see if it would be convenient to drop by.

These neighborly visits were welcomed for with the visitor came news of the day: Who had a new baby, who was sick and who had gone to the great beyond. There was no television, no good radio reception, and no cell phones. A quiet visit in the parlor with a cup of tea or just a glass of cool spring water was what grandmother had to offer. There was no iced tea or ice water because there was no electricity to make ice. Nor did Grandma have an icebox she could have stored it in.

Toward the end of the hallway to the right was the dining room where Grandmother displayed her skills in cookery. Grandad ate blackberry cobbler there, his favorite, with fresh cream poured over it. This became my favorite as well. Picking these berries at the mountain place with my Grandpop was a high point in my summer there. Our contests of seeing which of us could eat the most corn on the cob were special.

I have grandmother's round oak table and serving table at our deck house in Conyers, Georgia. The craftsman who beautifully restored this furniture said it was made in the late 1800s. This was when my grandparents were wed.

A door at the end of the hallway led directly into the kitchen, with the woodstove where Grandmom worked her magic. A few pounds added with each of her fifteen pregnancies saw that she became rather stout. However, this lady could move faster around her kitchen than anyone I have ever seen as she served meals to eight people three times a day. I was proud to keep her stovewood box full.

There was a back porch off of the kitchen where stairs led to the basement. Uncles Jack and John had piped spring water into a traceway (a large concrete pan) which was Grandmom's refrigerator. Milk and other foods were placed in large crocks and the cool water flowing around the vessels kept the food from spoiling.

At the top of the stairs straight ahead was a bedroom with three single beds that were occupied by me and uncle John and uncle Jack during that summer of adventure. I loved the little porch off our bedroom. We could view the apple house, the barn and grandma's vegetable and herb gardens from there. Uncle Hershel slept in the bedroom to the left and aunt Jessie Boone had the privacy of the bedroom to the right.

After Grandad and Grandma passed away, shutters were added to the house and the front porch was enclosed to become a sun porch. Uncle Charles and aunt Lorena Duckett made one large room out of the parlor and dining room and added a fireplace.

I am proud of the old home place and the way that cousin Kenny Duckett and his wife Gail have kept it in prime condition. It is a centerpiece of our Rogers family heritage.

5

THE DAY TILLIE'S PUPPIES DIED

THE SUMMERS that I spent on my grandparents' farm were a great blessing to me. I learned a lot about life and that there were many happy days down on the farm, but there were a few sad days, and this was one of them.

I was ten years old. There were no other children in the household, so Tillie, the cow dog, became my best friend. When I was outside, and that was most of the time, Tillie was by my side.

Tillie was a cattle dog, a working dog, who was born to go after the cows and bring them to the barn for milking, which had to occur twice a day. She loved her job and did it well, for she knew to not make the cows run, for this would make the cows hold up their milk.

Like a good dog, Tillie walked the cows from the pasture to the barn. A good supply of milk was important then, and grandmother would convert some of the milk to butter, and cottage cheese, and there would be cream for whipping and pouring generously on the blackberry cobblers.

In an era before my summer on the farm in 1939, livestock was allowed to graze free range. The crops were fenced to keep the livestock out, instead of the livestock being fenced in, therefore granddad's livestock freely mixed with his neighbors' cattle and they grazed wherever they wanted to.

Granddad Rogers had a dog named Ole Billy who was trained to go out on the free range and sort out only granddad's cattle and bring them back to the Rogers' barn. He never delivered the neighbors' cows to our granddad's barn.

One day, there was a big storm that struck the Rogers farm and there were some baby chickens that almost drowned. Ole Billy picked them up gently in his mouth and delivered them to the hearth of the fireplace to warm up and dry out. Just doing his job.

Granddad could say to Billy, "Poor Ole Billy has a headache, poor Ole Billy," and Billy would moan and rub his head with his paws. Needless to say, granddad Rogers was good at training animals.

Ole Billy was probably a great, great, etc. grandfather of Tillie. Farmers greatly valued their farm dogs and recognized the good bloodlines of these working dogs. The dogs owned by farmers on Crabtree Creek were similar and interbred. They looked a lot like Australian Shepherds and a little like Lassie, the famous dog in the movies.

The dogs were never spayed so there were frequent litters of puppies. Puppies were offered to friends and neighbors, and a farmer would sometimes keep the "pick of the litter" for a backup replacement of the principal cow dog. The second summer that I was on the Rogers' farm, a puppy named Major was kept as a future replacement of Tillie.

Major standing on a stump. The apple house is behind him to the right and the hay barn is at the left rear of the photo, with the big door leading to nowhere.

There was a limit on the number of dogs a farmer could afford to feed, so obviously most of the litters had to go. My Uncle Hershel was chosen to be the villain on this day.

Hershel put the puppies in a tow sack and went down to Crabtree Creek to do what had to be done, and this was the most humane method available. There was no Humane Society to share the blame. I knew that this was necessary, a part of the farm life of that time. However, this did not dull the pain of losing my little friends.

I know that I cried, but boys were not supposed to cry. Girls could cry, but boys had to be strong and just suck it up. Boys did not cling to their mommas and cry their hearts out. That would be sissy, and no self-respecting boy wanted to be a sissy in those days.

If a boy cried, he had to cry alone where nobody could see or hear him cry—that's just the way it was. I probably went out to the barn and climbed up to the hayloft to cry. No one could hear the man-child crying there. No one would know.

On the happy days, Tillie and I ran from the farmhouse to the barn, me with a cornstalk in my hand with Tillie tugging on the other end. Today, Tillie and the 10-year old boy walked slowly to the barn. Yes, Tillie and I cried that day.

6

BOYS WILL BE BOYS

GROWING up in Waynesville was a lot like growing up in the fictional town of Mayberry. We didn't have the friendly sheriff, but surely we had a lot of Opies and Aunt Bees, and there were lots of porches with swings. People generally watched out for each other and for all of the children.

There weren't drugs on Main Street, as there might be today —unless one considered the rumor that Jeff, who was the owner and druggist at the Waynesville Pharmacy, had availability to personal drugs. I worked for Jeff. He even gave me the keys to the store so I could open up when he didn't feel like coming in. He was kind and gentle man who extended this trust to me.

There was a Black man who also worked for Jeff. Alonzo was the first Black man I had ever known, and he was an Albino. Alonzo was always very polite, and with the starched white jacket he wore, looked more like a druggist than Jeff.

There were not many Black people in Waynesville, and they had their own separate school a few blocks off of Main Street on Pigeon Street. There were not separate water fountains, however. Everyone shared the water fountains on Main Street, which were built of creek rocks and ran the cool mountain water continuously for everyone to enjoy. There were no water shortages then, and Main Street was washed frequently by a washer truck with this same cool clear mountain water.

Everyone frequented the Waynesville Theatre on Main Street, since there were no videos and televisions. There was a separate entrance for the Black customers on the second floor, which was accessed by metal stairs on the side of the building. There was a ticket taker who sat just inside this entrance for the Black people who sat in the balcony. It was his duty to go down to the theatre entrance to change the billing on the marquis between the movie features.

A good friend of mine, Billy Richeson, and I figured that a good way to enjoy a movie for free would be to slip in the Colored entrance when it was left unattended, then just go downstairs and find a seat.

Bill and I both played trombone in the Waynesville Township Band under the tutorship of band director Charles Isley, who went on to head the music department at Appalachian State University. Bill also was a co-editor of the *Campus News*, along with Aaron Hyatt (Dr.), George "Wally" Brown (Dr.), Tommy "Jeep" Norris (deceased) and myself. We called ourselves "The Big Five." No inflated egos here!

The Big Five.

We ran off our newspaper copies on a duplicating machine under the direction of Mrs. Richeson, Bill's mother, who ran the school office and was secretary to the school principal.

Bill and I shared experiences as members of a high school fraternity, with exclusive features patterned after college frats, even with blackballing. Bill played on the high school football team and I played on the basketball team. Bill was later class president.

After Bill and I slipped into the movie house and were settled down enjoying the movie, a man came in and sat down beside Bill. We immediately recognized him as the ticket taker from the upstairs entrance.

He just sat there, saying nothing, while Bill and I began to sweat and worry about what he would do. Would he kick us out and make a public spectacle or have us arrested? Or what? This war of nerves went on for a while.

"Billy, don't do this again," he finally whispered.

The man lived down the street from Bill and knew him, but maybe Bill did not know him. Hillary Clinton has written *It*

Takes a Village, and I suppose some of that applies here. I admire the way that the man handled this little issue, with respect and dignity. Of course, Bill and I would never do this again, and we both learned from the experience.

How would this be handled today? Would our reputations have been ruined? Or would the commonsense knowledge and judgment of this mountain man have been applied, because he knew that "boys will be boys?"

7

DON'T BURN DOWN THE TOBACCO BARN

Smoking was the cool thing to do back in the Great Depression. President Franklin Delano Roosevelt smoked with his cigarette in a long cigarette holder. Hollywood actors and actresses always smoked in the movies.

The working man bought his tobacco in little cloth bags with a drawstring, and rolled his own. He could buy little packs of cigarette papers to roll his tobacco into a cigarette with the paper twisted at the end to keep from losing any tobacco. If he felt a little prosperous, he might purchase some Prince Albert tobacco in a can.

Kids back in the day would call their local store and play one of their favorite pranks.

"Do you have Prince Albert in a can?" they'd ask.

If the answer came back in the affirmative, the kid would say, "You'd better let him out, or he'll smother to death!" Then they'd squeal with laughter as they hung up the phone. So much for the humor of the day.

Kids would sometimes go out into the fields and find a plant that we called "rabbit tobacco." Smoking this plant was a daring and naughty thing to do to flaunt authority and keep this a secret from our parents. Of course, these little outlaws had to sneak into the kitchen and bootleg some matches and a paper bag for rolling paper.

One day me and my buddies were feeling a bit reckless and wanted to be big shots. We got some of the real tobacco that was curing in the tobacco barn, and were smoking our homemade cigarettes and being cool when Dad happened on the scene.

We had been caught red-handed. We quickly extinguished our cigarettes and awaited punishment for our audacious crime.

Dad asked me to come up to the house. We sat in the living room. He didn't lecture me about the evils of smoking.

"Ray," he said calmly, "if you're going to smoke, do it right here. We don't want you boys to burn down the tobacco barn."

The words that I heard from my dad that day were words from a wise man, who knew how to guide his children without threats or whipping. In his quietly modulated but stern voice, he only had to say, *We don't want you boys to burn down the tobacco barn.*

8

ALL WAS NOT WELL IN MAYBERRY

BACK IN THE forties I was a man about town. At thirteen, I had worked at the Dixie Home Store stocking grocery shelves for twenty-five cents an hour.

As I grew older, I became manager of the soda fountain at the Waynesville Pharmacy. They called us guys soda jerks. The new Winn Dixie Store paid more, so I moved across Main Street to work in the meat department. I learned how to be a butcher.

I never asked Mother and Dad for money. I had more than enough to go to movies, buy my own clothes and do whatever teenagers did in those days. What was left over I put in Mom's Bank.

Mom and Dad let me come and go as I pleased. I generally behaved myself.

One night, I was out a bit late and I was walking up Main Street. Our little town of Waynesville was kind of like Mayberry. We respected the town police, which we referred to as "The Law."

Main Street was not as well lit then as it is today, but that didn't bother me. I had never had any run-in with the law, and never thought that I would. I thought of policemen (no police women then) as being like the Mayberry police chief Andy Griffith and his sidekick Barney Fife.

That night, I learned that all was not well in Mayberry. As I approached the movie theater, I heard noises that wasn't supposed to be there. I cautiously made my way toward the theater entrance. The Marquee lights were out, so the late movie must have been over.

I realized that the noise coming from the alcove sounded like a fight. But it wasn't really a fight. It was a beating. I immediately, recognized the policeman. His initials were A.P.E., so he got the nickname "Ape." He'd been a football hero in high school.

His back was to me and he didn't know that anyone was watching. He didn't know that I saw him drive his fist into the stomach of the frail-looking farm boy with such force that the boy spit up blood.

I had seen enough. The boy and his friend were not resisting. There was no way they could. I suddenly realized that if the officer knew what I'd seen, I might be the next victim. I walked quickly away from the scene and my steps leading me toward home came a little faster than usual that night.

What should I do? I wondered. Whatever I said would be the word of a teenager against the word of a football hero and lawman. Who would believe me?

I thought about telling my Dad, but I knew that he might feel compelled to report this incident to the police chief. Then my Father might be a victim, and one day I might find his mangled body, or he might just disappear.

I decided to tell no one. I would hide this grisly scene in the farthest reaches of my mind. And I did. I hid it there, until one day recently it bubbled to the surface. I told my son Bradford about the beating.

I never saw anything in the Waynesville Mountaineer newspaper about any beatings. It was probably never reported.

I wondered what could these boys possibly have done to deserve this brutal treatment? They were not resisting arrest. Maybe this was an isolated incident. Maybe not.

I do know that several years later, after I left Waynesville for college, the football hero became Chief of Police.

9

WHAT, NO CREDIT SCORE?

CHILD LABOR LAWS did not prevent me from earning wages at age twelve or thirteen while working in a grocery store on Main Street. Later on I worked at the Waynesville Pharmacy, eventually managing the soda fountain. I suppose that my job title was a "soda jerk," but today the last part of the title engenders some resentment.

My early work career also involved mowing lawns and delivering newspapers while riding on the running board of a car belonging to my employer Mr. Joe Liner. Joe would knock on my window about 2:00 a.m. to wake me up. I would jump into my clothes and run to his auto, and we would drive to Charlie's Place, an all night hamburger restaurant, to meet the Asheville Citizen paper truck.

We delivered over four hundred newspapers in the towns of Waynesville and Hazelwood. When we finished the paper route and returned to my home about 6:00 a.m., I jumped into bed for about an hour's nap, getting up again at 7:00 a.m. to milk the cows before it was time to catch the school bus. One day I forgot to clean my shoes after milking the cows and got on the bus with smelly shoes. Not a good thing.

But, I digress...back to the paper route. Yes, I rode on the outside of the car, even if it was raining or snowing. I folded the papers and threw them onto the porches of our customers' houses. Sometimes I missed the porch and the paper would sail up on the roof of the porch. I guess Joe got cussed out when the paper was found on the roof.

I bought my own clothes and books and paid for my recreation, but I saved a lot of my wages and I deposited them in what I call Mom's Savings Bank.

These savings came in handy when my older brother Dean needed an operation. We had no insurance for the operation, for in those times most people had no medical coverage. My mother owned a little house which her father had given her. Today we would call it a shack, but I'm proud to say I was born in that shack.

My mother offered to sell me the little house, with the deposits in Mom's Savings Bank to be the downpayment. I would have to finance the balance to pay for Dean's operation. With some trepidation, this sixteen-year-old went down to the Haywood County Savings and Loan Association office to discuss financing this purchase. Surprisingly, they took me seriously and agreed to meet me at the house to further discuss the transaction.

As my memory serves me, three or four gentlemen drove up to the little house in a fine new automobile. (Maybe it was a Packard or a Pontiac, but it was an above the average-type vehicle). Here I was, a skinny sixteen-year-old meeting with these successful leaders of the community. They looked the house over and told me that they would give me the money. We closed the deal with a handshake.

Did they ask for my credit score? No, there was no such thing at that time. Did they run a credit check? No, most people paid cash or bartered goods or services then. I don't believe credit cards existed for most people then. Some people paid their bills by check, but most people just dealt with cash.

Did the Federal government require us to sign a stack of papers? No, I probably signed one piece of paper. Life was uncomplicated at the time. If the government had been involved then as they are today, I couldn't have gotten jobs and saved money at such an early age, and there is probably no way I could have obtained a loan from a financial institution.

Of course, I paid off the loan from the rental income without missing a payment. But how did these men decide that I was credit worthy?

I think I can tell you. They looked across the street and saw the nice little home of my grandfather, John Burnett Medford. They probably said, "Well, John Burnett owns several rental houses and he always pays his debts." They probably knew that he owned stock in the Farmers' Federation Co-op. Actually, I owned some too.

Then they looked across the little creek (some called it a branch) and there was school principal Frank Rogers' house. They probably said "Frank doesn't make a lot of money, but he is known to pay his debts. Then there's John Rogers, this boy's other grandfather, who owns a nice farm down on Crabtree Creek. He pays his debts too. This boy has saved enough for a downpayment at his early age, so I reckon he'll pay off this loan, just like his folks would do."

At that time, people were judged a lot by the conduct of the family they belonged to. People wanted to uphold the family name. Families with a good reputation were said to be from good stock.

The bottom line is this: My family's reputation was my credit score.

10

IT WAS ALL WINSTON'S FAULT

THE BRITISH high command decided that it was inevitable that the Germans would defeat the armies of Britain, Belgium and the Netherlands; and France fought a rearguard action to slow the German army as it flooded into their territory.

The British were ordered to evacuate from the port at Dunkirk. Every form of floating watercraft headed across the English Channel on May 28th, 1940 to rescue the trapped soldiers. As the Germans bombed, shelled and strafed the fleeing men, many boats went down.

The Brits pulled their comrades from the chilling waters to continue the retreat, and they planned to fight again on another day. It was nothing short of a miracle that by May 31, 1940 those 338,000 troops crossed the English Channel to the relative safety beyond the White Cliffs of Dover.

After the ignominious defeat, Winston Churchill stepped into the breach to bring the right words to rally the forces of the Western World. He faced reality on May 13th as he offered only *blood, toil, tears and sweat* to his countrymen.

On June 4th he spoke to England, to the USA, to Germany,

and to the rest of the world. His voice had a guttural tone and he was almost growling as the English bulldog delivered his message from his lair.

We shall fight on the beaches, we shall fight on the landing ground, we shall fight in the fields and in the streets...in the hills. We shall never surrender. As the Western World rallied to his words, he stated on June 18, 1940 that *this was our finest hour.*

This ten-year old boy heard Winston and he understood. And the stage was set.

Mrs. Kellett, my Latin teacher, long a fixture of Waynesville Township High School, sometimes tended to stray from the teaching of Latin into something akin to hero worship of the Romans. And so it came to pass that Mrs. Kellett stated that the Roman Emperor Julius Caesar was the greatest man who ever lived.

Unknowingly, she had thrown down the gauntlet and challenged one of her students.

I could not let this stand.

"No, No, Mrs. Kellett, Julius is not the greatest. Winston Churchill is the greatest," I declared.

Then I began to lay out my case that Winston and his well-chosen words had saved our Western World.

When Mrs. Kellett's face turned red and a few of my classmates began to snicker, I knew that I had stepped into something that would not bode well.

My feelings were confirmed when the report cards came out. I got an "F." My Dad, a long time teacher and school principal, viewed my report card and inquired about the F. I had never before received one.

I told him my story as he tried to hold his stern demeanor. Knowing Mrs. Kellett and her tendencies, he finally broke out laughing.

And now, the rest of the story.

I later enrolled in Mars Hill College and they required completion of two years of foreign language. So to make up for the deficiency, I enrolled in a Spanish class.

Well, for those of you who feel that life is not fair, it came to pass that I got the best looking redheaded Spanish teacher North of the Rio Grande. Hey, I even enrolled in her Spanish Club.

Even though this little story has an undeserved happy ending, I still contend that it was all Winston's fault. That's my story and I'm going to stick to it!

11

THE DEATH OF GRANT PARROTT

ONE DAY when I was about sixteen, my cousin Bill Parrott came running down Hall Top Road, which ran up to Aunt Ruth's house.

"Something's wrong with my Daddy!" he shouted.

His father was Grant Parrott, who had married Mother's sister Ruth after her first husband had died.

I ran all the way up to Aunt Ruth's house, and found her on the front porch anxiously wringing her hands. Grant Parrott was seated in a rocking chair with his eyes closed and his head slumped down on his chest.

I tried to find his pulse, but found none. I put my head to his chest, but couldn't detect a heartbeat.

"I believe he's dead," I said to Aunt Ruth.

There was almost no reaction from Ruth. She didn't cry, and why would she?

Grant Parrott had been cruel to her and to their six children. He usually behaved himself when he was sober, but when he drank he became a different person. He had threatened my grandfather, John Burnett Medford. He'd also threatened my father. Grant Parrott's threats were taken seriously since it was rumored—but not proven—that he had killed his first wife and buried her under a slab of concrete at their home in another county.

One of his children said that during some of his tirades, they would run out of the house into the bushes and hide, until he passed out drunk.

I felt no remorse in his passing, only sympathy for Aunt Ruth and a surge of gratitude that she would at last be free. Somehow I carried the dead body into the house and placed it on a bed. Grant Parrott was a man of average height and build, but I was just a teenager.

I felt a twinge of guilt, since my religion taught me that all life is sacred. *Should I feel bad about his death?* I wondered. But my attention soon turned to my cousins, who were crying.

As time passed, Aunt Ruth began to come out of the shell she'd built around herself. With my Dad's considerable assistance, she was able to get Social Security benefits. But before she could receive any money, Grant Parrott's first wife had to officially be declared deceased—and she had simply disappeared and her body was never found.

Later on, two of Ruth's sons (Eddie and Jack) who were excellent carpenters built her a nice little home on land that Granddad Medford had given her. She found peace there, and lived out her allotted years in her new home, putting away the life she lived with Grant Parrott in the old decaying house down the hill.

PART II

MORE MOUNTAIN TECHNOLOGY

12

THE LAZY GIRL

Great-grandfather Eldridge Medford lived here with his wife Mary Ann Rogers Medford.

RUBEN ELDRIDGE MEDFORD came home from the Great War between the states in May, 1865, having been a prisoner of war at Camp Douglas, Illinois.

Eldridge said his general had sold out to the Yankees and his company had been ordered to surrender and stack arms.

General Frazier went to Boston afterwards, perhaps knowing that if he stayed in the southland, his life would not be worth a Confederate dollar.

Eldridge threw his gun down the mountain as far as he could and did not stack his arm as instructed. He said that he "didn't plumb surrender." He was a proud and independent mountaineer.

Captain Asbury Thornton Rogers had also been imprisoned after the Confederate surrender at Cumberland Gap, September 9, 1863. He spent his time in the Louisville Military Prison at Johnson Island until June 12, 1865.

Asbury had a sister named Mary Ann, and Eldridge chose her to be his bride and they were married in 1866. They moved into a log cabin, which is still standing down the ridge from the house once owned by my great uncle Robert French (Bob) Rogers, who was a son of Asbury.

My great grandfather Eldridge (on my mother's side of the family) was a very religious man never saying a curse word stronger than darn. Els (a nickname) belonged to the Southern Methodist Church and it has been said that every time that the church doors were opened that he would be there. He always voted a straight Democrat ticket.

All of this having been said, Els had a lazy girl on the premises. Strange as it may seem, Mary Ann approved of the lazy gal and even found her to be quite helpful while raising their two small children at this location.

Mary Ann Rogers Medford and Eldridge had eight children together (in spite of this lazy girl having been present early in their marriage). After Mary Ann passed away, Eldridge then married Mary Ann Russell and they had a second family including six additional children.

It is a wise man indeed who chooses a second wife with the

same name as his first wife. There is no possibility of inadvertently calling the second wife the first wife's name.

In those days houses had to be located near a water source such as a spring, or a well had to be dug. There were no water systems to hook up to out in rural America. However, these pioneers were very inventive in building devices to make their lives a little easier.

Eldridge had a problem. The spring nearest his cabin was down a steep slope. This hillside would have been very difficult to climb carrying a bucket or two of water even if it was not soggy wet or covered with ice or snow.

My great grandfather could build just about anything from a fine piece of walnut furniture, a loom, a cupboard, or even a chimney. He built the chimneys at the Lorena Davis/Asbury Thornton Rogers house. He constructed a little satchel made of oak wood with brass trim and even a lock while in prison, in which to carry his meager belongings.

Eldridge constructed a rope and pulley device to fetch water from the spring up to his and Mary Ann's cabin. Yep, you guessed it; this clever device is called a lazy girl. Well, I reckon you can now see how Mary Ann would tolerate having a lazy girl on the premises.

13

THE COAL BUCKET

WHAT IS A COAL BUCKET? If you were born after about 1950, you probably don't have a clue.

When the icy cold winter winds blew through the cracks of the wood siding and penetrated the beaded tongue and groove wood that covered the inside walls of the Rogers home in Hanging Dog, we needed something to keep us warm.

The wood-fired cook stove in the kitchen kept that area of the house cozy, and an oil-fired stove in the dining room, which doubled as a den in the winter, heated another area of our house. There was no central heating system and the walls were not insulated. The only means of heating the front bedroom and the living room were the fireplaces.

My dad had coal grates installed in the fireplaces of the front bedroom and the living room. These coal grates were designed to hold the coal a few inches off of the floor of the fireplace to allow air to circulate up through the burning coal.

Coal burned hotter than wood and it was difficult to keep enough wood cut to fuel the kitchen stove plus the fireplaces. Coal was ordered and a coal truck dumped a large pile of coal up beside Hall Top Road, which ran by the upper side of our house.

This is where boy power and the coal bucket came into play. The coal bucket was not round in shape, as are most buckets that you are acquainted with. The coal bucket is almost triangular in shape with one side featuring a kind of spout sloping outward from bottom to the top of the vessel to allow the coal to be poured from the bucket into the grate in the fireplace.

Today, one might find a coal bucket in an antique shop for closer examination. Of course, there are photographs of a coal bucket, sometimes called a coal hod on Google. Coal hods are always painted black as coal and constructed of durable galvanized metal to retard rusting.

Boy power was used to go out to the coal pile right before bedtime to fill the bucket with coal, and lug the heavy vessel back into the house and hope that there would be enough coal to keep the fire burning into the night before it would die back.

When morning came and the bedroom was freezing, one would hope that there were a few live coals under the ashes in the fireplace to help get the fire going again. A few sticks of kindling wood helped the process.

Dad usually got the fires going early in the morning while the family still snuggled under the feather bed covers. But boy power soon came into play as the coal bucket needed to be filled again.

The ashes from the previous day needed to be removed from the fireplace and deposited outside. I remember brushing the snow from the lumps of coal before placing the lumps into the bucket and sometimes having to break the lumps apart when they would freeze together.

Folks who lived in towns and cities may have dealt with coal burning a bit differently. A lot of people lived in houses with basements with a coal shoot that allowed coal to be poured directly from a truck into the basement where a furnace waited to burn the black packages of energy. No piles of coal in the yards of these wealthier citizens.

Some had furnaces with boilers that supplied radiators with even heat throughout the cold of the nights. A downside might be the explosion of a poorly serviced boiler. Boiler insurance could even be purchased.

In the days of coal buckets, we were thankful for coal and the warmth that it brought to our homes. Little did we know that in a few decades coal would become a villain, deemed by many a principal cause of global warming. Coal mines would be closed down and politicians would argue the merits and demerits of coal.

Society turned to heat pumps and natural gas to provide needed warmth and coal buckets have become relics of the past, along with buggy whips, feather beds and glass bottles of milk sitting on doorsteps in the early morning hours.

14

NUMBER, PLEASE?

How long has it been since you heard a sweet feminine voice say "Number, please?" when you picked up a telephone?

Most of you have never heard these words, but if you lived in the 1930s and 1940s, this started the process of placing a telephone call. You gave the number that you wanted to reach to the operator at the exchange and she plugged in a cord that connected you with the desired number.

My first phone number, long after I moved from the mountains, was Melrose 2447. Yep, phone numbers had names. The exchange name "Melrose" indicated that my location was in Northeast Atlanta.

When someone said "Hello?" at the other end of the wire, the conversation could begin. Yes, there had to be a wire connecting you to the other party, even if it was all the way across the United States.

But your conversation may not have been private. The operator could listen in and you may have been hooked up to a party line. Everyone on the party line could hear the phone ring so anyone could pick up their phone and hear your conversation.

Each person on the party line had their own unique ring so everyone on the line knew when you received a call. Party lines were popular because they were much cheaper than private lines.

Maintenance of the wired network was very expensive. Just think of the number of telephone poles it took to string wires from Washington, D.C. to Los Angeles. Consequently, long distance calls were expensive and usually rather short and to the point. No idle taking and calling Momma every day

A friend told me that in the little town she lived in, she had to go to the telephone office to make a long distance call. This is difficult for us to visualize in this era of cellular telephones, when we can call anywhere at no extra charge.

When our family lived in Jupiter, I was in the fourth through the seventh grades, and we didn't have a phone in our home. When we moved from that rural area to Waynesville, we had no phone for quite a while.

When we finally had one installed, the people who lived up the Hall Top Road in Grandfather Medford's little rental houses came to our house to make their phone calls. We didn't mind. People tended to share and help others more in those days.

Alexander Graham Bell made the first phone call to his assistant Thomas Watson, who was in the next room, saying "Mr. Watson, come here. I want to see you." Watson came. A patent was issued in 1876.

When I was a child, we made primitive phones out of two tin cans with a hole in the bottom and a length of string connecting the cans. Actually, we could hear sound transmitted to the next room. I never got a patent on this device.

Phone booths began to appear at convenient locations in 1905 and became a significant aid in keeping in touch. Hubby could call his wife to find out if he needed to pick up a loaf of bread or a dozen eggs. A giant leap forward in the world of communication!

Cell phones came into our lives in 1980 and the phone booths began to gradually disappear. Mild-mannered Clark Kent could not find a phone booth to change into his Superman clothing and go flying about Metropolis to fight crime.

I know that most of you have wondered why you hadn't seen Superman lately and now the mystery has been solved. Lois Lane is also happy knowing why she had not seen the love of her life.

Once my sister Sara was on a trip with her husband John. Sara was napping on the back seat of their car when John pulled into a service station to refuel. While John was in the station paying for his fill-up, Sara went into the ladies room. John reentered the vehicle not looking in the back seat and continued on their journey.

Miles down the highway, John spoke to Sara. When there was no answer, John realized that Sara was missing. Meanwhile, Sara was waiting patiently for John to come back for her. If cell phones had been invented at this time, John's trip would have been shortened considerably and I would not be telling you this story about the wife who vanished.

Many of you have never used a rotary phone, since push button phones came along during the 1970s. The first rotary phones were large and heavy and they were always black. When colored phones became available, it was a big event. The ladies loved to be able to get phones to match the decor of their homes.

Cordless phones became popular in the 1990s, freeing some folks from being tethered to the phone cradle. Phone books have been with us since 1886, but are now almost obsolete, thanks to Google. Emergency 911 systems came to us in 1986, and have saved many lives.

But the biggie was the cellular phone coming our way in 1980. Everybody has to have one, and I will not attempt to list everything that can be accomplished with a smart phone. The smart phone has changed our lives—forever—even though it never says "Number, please?" when you turn it on.

15

CARS-R-US

RECENTLY I READ an article wherein a one hundred eleven-year-old Georgia lady stated that, during the three centuries her life had spanned, the two most important inventions to her were television and the automobile. America, no doubt, has a love affair with both.

To Granddad John Burnett Medford, it was love at first sight. There were no autos at all in Iron Duff Community when Granddad decided to drive some cattle to market. On the way to the cattle market, he met a man driving a T-model Ford.

John Burnett (he was always called by both names) was so taken by this new machine that he bought it right on the spot, and proceeded to drive it home. Never having had a driving lesson—and perhaps not even having ridden in a car before—he forgot how to stop Henry Ford's invention when he arrived back in Iron Duff.

What a dilemma! He had the good judgment to just drive it into a ditch. This stopped the car with no great damage to the vehicle. This experience must have affected him, because for all the time I knew him he did not own a car. So much for love at first sight.

Dad owned a car that most of you have never heard of, a four-cylinder Essex. He bought this car in 1926 and drove it to his teaching job at Liberty School near Jonathan Creek. Much of the time later that we lived in Waynesville, Dad did not own a car, but this was not unusual at this time.

During World War II, since we did not have an automobile, we didn't have to worry about the rationing of tires and gasoline. We just walked everywhere. Dad walked to East Waynesville School, where he was the principal. We all walked to church and to town, and if we missed the school bus we walked to school. I suppose shoe rationing was of some concern, but since us kids went barefoot all summer long, this wasn't a big problem.

After WWII was over, Dad obtained a war surplus Willy's Jeep, which was the vehicle that I learned to drive. Just after I got my license, I was driving the Jeep down an alley between two brick buildings in Waynesville. I scraped one of the buildings a little, but there were so many scrapes on the old Jeep that one more didn't make much difference. I don't remember telling Dad about this until now. Well, confession is good for the soul.

Dad also owned an Edsel, I believe this was in the fifties. The car was named for Edsel Ford, son of Henry Ford. At this time, pink and grey were in style with pink and grey tile in bathrooms, and even pink and grey automobiles. Dad bought a pink and grey Edsel, and he was really in high cotton with this fine automobile.

Around 1939, Uncle Bob Rogers owned one of only two vehicles in the Crabtree Community, which was a T-model Ford convertible touring car. One could visualize politicians of the day riding in this type vehicle waving to the crowds as the parade drove by. Great-uncle Bob was a real sport, right up to the day he drove his pickup truck over to the nursing home at age 95, where he lived until his death at age 99.

Uncle Weldon Willis was also a sport —maybe even the cat's meow—when he drove his Studebaker Golden Hawk to the Rogers Family reunion. Well, I was impressed anyway, as this vehicle was way ahead of its time with its sleek design.

Brother Mark served our country well as a member of the U.S. Army band stationed in Trieste, Italy. Mark had the good fortune of living in a castle while stationed there. He also had the good fortune of being able to purchase a 1949 Nash Ambassador for a good price.

This vehicle had the unusual feature, in that the back of the front seats would let down to make a bed. Mark decided not to bring this gem back to the U.S. of A. because he didn't believe it would endure the drive from New York to North Carolina. Mark parked the vehicle on the dock and as his troop ship pulled away he waved goodbye to his Ambassador.

A bit of trivia here: While Mark was in college at Western Carolina Teachers College (now a University) he had his own band, the Mark VI Jazz Combo. And now we fast forward two generations. At age seventeen, my Great nephew Zack Wade started his own band, the Random Blues.

And here is the neat part: Zack's band played from sheets of music handed down from Great-uncle Mark. Mark played a cool sax and Zack plays a hot trombone.

A good friend of mine and I pooled our resources when we were about sixteen or seventeen and bought an old LaSalle coupe for fifty dollars. The LaSalle was a fine automobile, probably considered the luxury class in its heyday.

We drove around and showed off for a few days until the LaSalle just quit on us. Seems as if the block was cracked when we bought it. The former owner had doctored it with some gunk to make it run while he sold it to a couple of suckers. I don't believe we had the title transferred, so we left it on the side of the road when it quit. Do you reckon the former owner had to pay for it to be towed away? Perhaps justice prevailed.

Much later in life, I purchased a replica 1929 Mercedes kit car. It was yellow with black fenders and chrome flex-pipes on each side of the motor. A real little classic sports convertible. I wanted my son, Bradford, to learn something about mechanics that I couldn't teach him.

Since I inherited Dad's lack of mechanical knowledge and expertise, I made a deal with my nephew Greg Hyatt, who had some time between quarters at college, to build the kit car. Well, Bradford would have none of this mechanic stuff, so all of Greg's mechanical expertise was never transferred to Bradford. You know what has been said about the best laid plans of mice and men.

Actually, Bradford later learned on his own how to make mechanical repairs on a couple of old vehicles that he once owned. He also works on the diesel engine of his nine ton sail-boat, so my wishes were not totally in vain.

Greg had restored a 1948 Willy's Overland Jeep to beautiful condition. While he was driving it, a North Carolina State Patrolman pulled him over. He was pleasantly surprised to learn that he had done nothing wrong and would not get a ticket. The patrolman just wanted to check out his cool pickup truck.

When Greg was a teenager, he bought two old Volkswagen bugs that didn't work. He used the best parts from each to build one Volkswagen that did work—except that the new creation didn't work in reverse. Just keep on trucking, Greg, with your newly built hot rod.

It has been said that one's personality is reflected in the type of vehicle they own. All of us have seen this from time to time. This leads me to explain that I really was not a hippie when I owned a Volkswagen camper. The ole soccer coach just used it to haul around little soccer players, who actually thought that it was cool. They really liked to hear the manual shift slow down the camper, as I geared it down for their benefit.

All of us have had cars that we loved, and some we loved to hate. There is no doubt that Americans have been greatly affected by the invention of the automobile, and that we Americans do indeed love our cars.

16

COLD MOUNTAIN AND THE LITTLE SATCHEL

CAMP DANIEL BOONE is at the foot of Cold Mountain. As a young Boy Scout enjoying my first camping experience at age twelve, I only know that the water in the little lake was extremely cold for swimming. When you first jumped in, it almost took your breath away. But it was fun to frolic in once your body adjusted to the temperature.

I didn't know that the camp was at the foot of Cold Mountain, nor did I know that the writer Charles Fraizer would one day pen a novel named *Cold Mountain* which would find the summit of the bestseller lists.

Charles Fraizer would be a friend of my sister, Jane Hyatt. Hollywood would make a film about a Confederate soldier making his way to his home on Cold Mountain as a survivor of this bloody conflict.

My great-grandfather, Ruben Eldridge Medford, also made the journey home from a prison camp (Camp Douglas) in Illinois. Els Medford spend one year, seven months and eleven days in this dastardly camp where almost half of those Confederate prisoners died of starvation, exposure and disease. They would even eat rats if they could trap them.

Their trip home had some similarities to the trip home of the soldier in the book *Cold Mountain*. On release from Camp Douglas, my great-grandfather was shipped by train to Morristown, Tennessee. It was up to him and the other captives to find their way across the dangerous Smoky Mountains to their homes in Haywood County. At this time, there were black bears and panthers in these mountains.

Eldridge carried a little satchel that he had made while in prison. It was made of oak with a curved top, and trimmed in brass. The Yankees discovered that Els (his nickname) was a skilled craftsman so they put him to work in a shop. He was able to hide the little suitcase under wood shavings produced by his work and prevent the item from being confiscated by his captors.

A woolen blanket somehow came to Eldridge while he was imprisoned, from his mother Nancy Colvard Medford. Eldridge was a skillful tailor as well as a carpenter, mason and maker of furniture and looms for weaving. He made a suit of clothes from the blanket and placed it in the satchel, awaiting his freedom.

After Els had made his way through the mountains and was near his home, he bathed in a stream to be sure that he was rid of lice from the prison camp. Sanitary conditions were so dismal in the prison compound that it was next to impossible to get rid of body lice.

He discarded his ragged prison clothes, opened his home-made suitcase, put on the clean suit he had made, and was able to come back to the waiting arms of his family as a proud man not beaten down by adversity. I remember my Mother wiping tears from her eyes as she told of her grandfather's hardships.

My cousin Mark Rogers has the little satchel well kept in the restored home of my great-grandmother, Lorena Davis Rogers. The home sits majestically overlooking 500 acres that once belonged to Confederate Captain Asbury Thornton Rogers. I am proud that this ancestral home and acreage is still in the Rogers family.

Yes, Eldridge's journey home was similar to the journey made in *Cold Mountain*, but there was no movie made about Els. We have our own "Cold Mountain" stories that will remain mostly untold because the little satchel cannot tell us.

17

THEY ARE AT REST IN THE ATTIC

As you passes through your busy life, sometimes you're attracted to particular items that become special to you. In my case, it was hand tools.

I suppose that Dad and Mother noticed that I liked to work with my hands and make things, so lo and behold, one Christmas I received a little tool kit, scaled to my size. I didn't have much wood to work with, so when a family sofa was junked, I salvaged a piece of plywood and made a little doll bed for my younger sister, Jane. There was pride in my accomplishment, and I think that Jane liked it.

The years passed swiftly by, and I was again attracted by hand tools as described in the *Foxfire* books. The *Foxfire* series told how our ancestors carved out their homes in the wilderness of the North Georgia mountains with unique hand tools.

I suppose you could say the *Foxfire* books rekindled a fire in my heart for tools., and started my quest to acquire antique hand tools. I began dropping by yard sales and flea markets and buying antique tools that were in good condition and could still be used. These tools were sturdily constructed to last a long time, maybe even a lifetime of a carpenter that treated the tools with the respect they deserved.

My niece Sharyn Hyatt-Wade noticed my tool collection, and as a teenager painted a watercolor of a few of my antique tools resting on the hearth of a fireplace that she and her father, Aaron Hyatt, had lovingly constructed together. Sheri later painted more tools for a matching set of paintings that hung in my office for over thirty years, where I would proudly point them out to my customers.

An older gentleman, maybe ninety years old, called my office and requested that I come to his home to discuss his insurance. I made a lot of visits to my customers' homes back in the day.

(Maybe this is a reason that many families stayed with my agency for over fifty years. I don't know if agent-client relationships will be as lasting in this age of technology. Probably not. But I digress.)

During our interview, I admired a hand-carved chest in his living room. He then showed me other pieces of his handiwork, and this led us to his basement workshop.

He showed me a little box that he had made for the most complicated wood plane that I had ever seen. It was manufactured by Stanley Rule and Level Company, and my customer had the original instruction booklet and multiple blades.

One could make any type of molding or trim with this tool. The gentleman saw that I was fascinated with the tool.

"Here, it's yours. I want you to have it," he said.

"I don't want you to give it to me. I might buy it from you."

"No, my nephew, who is my only heir, doesn't appreciate it. You do. And I want you to have it," he said, putting the box in my hands.

I spent that evening examining and playing with this very unique instrument which I later discovered was quite valuable. I showed it to my son, Bradford, who admired it, so it is now his to cherish.

The years have slipped by and I am now eighty-nine. My love for hand tools is still strong, but my days of collecting tools diminished long ago. I placed them one by one to rest in a trunk in the attic, waiting to be loved and cherished by some traveler passing through this amazing creation.

PART III

MORE GOOD EATS

18

MOTHERS OF AMERICA, ARISE!

WHEN PIONEER FAMILIES made their way into the wilderness to find a new life, there was most always a butter manufacturing machine tied to the back of the wagon.

It was called a cow, a necessity in those days. Butter was on every table, and was needed to fry eggs in on frosty mornings and to eat with sorghum syrup and biscuits. It is amazing the number of recipes that call for butter.

How well I remember, back in the thirties and even into the forties, my grandmother sitting in a ladder back chair with a churn in front of her working the dasher up and down.

Soon she would make the clobbered milk turn into butter and, lest we forget, delicious buttermilk. Freshly churned buttermilk we drank in those times was much more tasty than the buttermilk we now buy in our grocery stores.

Before the advent of electricity, the butter, after being pressed into decorative designs by a butter press, was placed in a crock in the spring house or lowered into a cool well for keeping. However, the butter print always found its way to the dining table for every meal, maybe to slather on a biscuit or a slice of cornbread. And what would an ear of corn fresh from the boiling pot taste like without plenty of melted butter?

For the city folks and the townspeople, who did not own a cow, butter became increasingly expensive. This circumstance encouraged American ingenuity to kick in, and our scientists invented a new product called margarine.

Margarine could be manufactured much cheaper than butter, but it was white, looking much like lard. No one wanted to put a substance that looked like lard on a biscuit or contaminate their sourwood honey with this unappetizing product.

There was nothing left to do but to color margarine yellow like butter. The dairy industry became greatly troubled by the competition threatened by this cheaper product that looked like and acted like butter. Dairy farmers feared the price of butter dropping and their profits declining.

Consequently, the Dairy Lobby kicked into action! The farmers collared their congressmen, and soon Congress passed a law that made it unlawful to sell colored margarine. Down with competition and back to white, lard-like margarine.

Well, good ole American ingenuity kicked in again, and little plastic pellets of liquid yellow color were placed in every package of margarine. Mothers all around America then had another chore added to their busy lives. They now had the privilege of coloring their margarine.

This little chore was passed down to the children in the family, who broke the yellow pellets of color and kneaded the color into the margarine. This was not easily done, and getting the color evenly distributed took considerable effort. Soon the children tired of this novelty and this became an unwanted chore, both by mothers and their children.

The power of American mothers should never be underestimated. The time had come. It was the time for American mothers to arise!

The American Dairy Lobby thought they were almighty, but their power was soon diminished by American motherhood. When congressmen came back from Washington to their districts, a fury was dispatched upon them. *How dare you add another chore to our busy lives?*

"We want colored margarine!" was the cry from the hinterlands.

Soon these powerful congressmen were dispatched back to Washington with their tails between their legs. The Dairy Lobby was no match.

When American mothers arise, to heck with high priced butter, and down with white, lard-like margarine. To heck with another unwanted, unneeded chore!

It was no contest. American Motherhood won again as colored margarine again populated our countryside. Three cheers for American Motherhood!

19

MY DAD'S APPLE TREES

SOMETIME DURING THE winter or early spring months, the seed catalogs would arrive at our house via the U.S. Post Office. This was the time to plan the garden for the coming year.

During the Great Depression, vegetable gardens were not planned as a recreational event or a hobby. For most families who lived in the Western North Carolina Mountains, gardens were a necessity.

Of course, the Victory gardens were encouraged by our leaders during World War II, and many people who lived in towns dutifully raised some of their own food.

Planting, tending and harvesting the vegetables was a family affair, although Dad did most of the heavy lifting, so to speak. The garden plot had to be plowed, and it seems there was always somebody who lived nearby who owned a mule or horse who could do the job.

Maybe Dad would just borrow the mule and plow and do the job himself, since he grew up on a farm and knew their skills. When the garden "came in," Dad might take the owner of the mule a "mess" of vegetables in payment for the plowing. This was how it worked, neighbor helping neighbor.

Let's just follow one item in our garden through the complete cycle from planting to a delicious dish on mother's table. Naturally (pun intended), fertilizer was removed from the barn and spread on the garden area before the plowing was initiated if one wanted a flourishing garden.

For sweet potatoes, Dad would lay out the rows and the soil would be mounded up. The youngest family member would walk along the row and drop the potato slips (young plants) with predetermined spaces between the plants to allow proper development of the potatoes.

Another family member would follow next to install the little plants carefully with a bowl-like space around the plant that would hold water. Then, buckets of water would be carried from a nearby branch (a small creek) and each plant would receive a generous share.

During the growing season, the natural fertilizer from the barn also made the weeds flourish, so pulling weeds became a necessary chore. The potatoes grew and the vines covered the mounds until fall approached and they began to die.

Now comes the harvest. The last of life for which the first was lived, to borrow a phrase.

Care must be taken in removing the sweet potatoes from the mounds, because a cut or scrape on the potato might cause spoilage or rotting during the winter storage. After a short drying period, the potatoes were carefully wrapped in newspaper, placed in cardboard boxes and stored in the attic above the kitchen where they would not freeze. There was a fire in the kitchen stove every day and the heat rose into the attic.

Now comes the good part. Any time our family had a hankering for sweet potatoes, they were readily available.

Sometimes we might want the long and slender white sweet

potatoes, a variety preferred for baking by many mountain families. Other times, Mother would choose the chubbier yellow variety, which was good for candied potatoes. They were sliced and cooked with brown sugar that made a syrup that appropriately complimented the lowly potato.

To be sure, the kids in the family got their rewards for helping in the garden when Mother cooked her sweet potato casserole with delicately browned marshmallows on top.

I don't remember this working and sweating in the garden as drudgery. There was laughing, teasing and joking as we worked together as a family. Today we might call it bonding, but then we never even knew the meaning of the word.

As I recall, Dad received a publication from Stark Nurseries from which Dad ordered a variety of apple trees. When the tiny trees arrived, they didn't look so good to me and I wondered if they would live. But my Dad had more faith than I.

I suppose that I was about thirteen when the duty fell to me to plant these scrubby little apple trees. Following my Dad's instructions, I made trips to the barnyard for what the cows contributed to this noble endeavor. I dug large holes, and this material was worked into the loose soil.

These trees, which were properly planted along the little creek which ran along the lower side of the garden, flourished—and Dad's visions, when he looked at the nursery catalogue, were abundantly fulfilled.

Over the years, Dad harvested bushels of apples from these trees. He put them in storage at the Francis Orchard facility, and withdrew them a bushel at a time. He relished the opportunity to give apples to family and friends, and when I visited Mom and Dad in the winter months, I always left with a bag of apples.

Our mother spread happiness to our family as she put before us her famous clear apple jelly (you could almost see through it), apple cobbler to kill for, stewed apple slices in a sweet sauce, apple turnovers made from dried apples, apple butter, and the not-to-be-forgotten apple sauce layer cake.

This cake became the wedding cake for my niece Sharyn Hyatt Wade, granddaughter of Frank and Willie Boone Rogers. It seems that Mother would create miracles with just a few apples and a lot of talent.

Memories of Dad sitting by the oil stove, peeling an apple on a chilly winter evening with his bare feet on the cold, wooden floor (he always removed his socks) will forever be cherished. May his children, his grandchildren and his great grandchildren and even additional generations know this, for this is our heritage.

20

LUCY'S CORNBREAD DRESSING, OR JOHN BURNETT'S CHICKEN BREAD

HERE IS a recipe for Lucy's cornbread dressing. It tastes like what mom used to make. Lucy has never actually baked this dressing from a recipe... it was just in her head.

I have helped her for several years by doing the chopping and crumbling, but she has always been the brains behind this operation. I decided that this year would be a good time to get this delicious recipe into written form.

Grandpa John Burnett called this product "chicken bread." Back in the day, we killed a big fat hen for Thanksgiving, thus "chicken bread." We made our own chicken broth, but you folks will have to buy some. You may have to cut back the size of the recipe. Well, good luck and send me some.

Love, Ray Baby

Lucy's Cornbread Dressing, or John Burnett's Chicken Bread

Cook 2 cakes of cornbread in a 12 inch iron skillet (no sugar or flour!) the day before you cook the dressing. Make the cakes about 2 inches thick so that there is not too much crust. Put 3 eggs in each pan of batter.

Save some cornbread batter to bake later.

Chop 1 large celery bunch (about 3 cups) Chop about 3 cups of onions. Chop 2 bunches of shallots including green tops (about 2 cups)

Sauté above with 1 stick of butter.

Crumble the cornbread to a fine texture in a large pan and mix in 10 chopped hard boiled eggs. Mix sautéed onions, shallots, and celery into crumbled cornbread, along with 2 raw eggs.

Mix 1 can (10 ½ oz.) each of cream of celery, cream of chicken, and cream of mushrooms into saucepan, heat while stirring in about 12 oz. of chicken broth. Mix into pan of cornbread crumbs while gradually adding 36 oz. of chicken broth. Add black pepper, sage, basil, and salt to taste. Stir well and pour into baking pans. Bake at 350 degrees until brown.

21

THE WAYNESVILLE RAMP CONVENTION

My Webster's *New Collegiate Dictionary*, published in 1956, defines a ramp as "an inclined plane," and highway departments worldwide have installed ramps to exit or access our highways. Somehow, Mr. Webster and his learned associates failed to identify a pungent vegetable that grows in the Great Smoky Mountains. Similar wild leeks grow as far north as Minnesota.

Mountaineers in the distant past considered the ramp, an odoriferous relative of the onion, to be an excellent spring tonic, bringing vitamins and minerals to a population deprived of fresh vegetables and fruits over the long winter months.

In the 1920s, the North Carolina Society of the Friends of the Ramp was formed to hold festivals or conventions to honor the ramp (*Allium Tricoccum*). The ramp now apparently has many friends since Ramp Conventions are held all throughout the Appalachian Mountain region.

Politicians soon recognized that hundreds of people attended these gatherings to enjoy ramp recipes and some good ole mountain hoedown music.

North Carolina Secretary of the State Thad Eure was invited to speak to the convention in the late 1930s and soon was chosen King of the Ramps. He filled this position for more than 50 years until his death on July 21, 1993. Governors and other high ranking politicians have regularly attended these functions.

The convention was held at Black Camp Gap for many years, but in 1953, construction of the Blue Ridge Parkway made Black Camp Gap inaccessible.

The convention was also held at Camp Hope for a while. American Legion Post #47 began hosting the gathering in 1968 and they now hold the event at the Post Home on Legion Drive in Waynesville. 2007 was the 73rd anniversary of this particular ramp convention.

The ramp is harvested in the wild in late April thru early May. Due to its popularity, the U.S. Government has banned its harvest on public lands to prevent overharvesting to preserve the plant.

However, this rare delectable plant can now be purchased online at earthy.com. Prestige restaurants and chefs have discovered the ramp and have added their own recipes to menus across the country. Even Mr. Webster may now be aware of the ramp.

Who could have imagined that the folk medicine reputation of the ramp would turn out to be well deserved? It has been discovered that the ramp has high levels of Vitamin C and A, and is full of healthful minerals. Ramps have the same cholesterol-reducing capacity of garlic, a close cousin. Oregon State University is conducting research regarding the cancer-preventing potential of the ramp.

There is a story about some high school boys rubbing the stinky ramp on the school radiators, closing the school for the day. It is said that the ramp will prevent colds, and this may be correct. If nobody comes near you, I reckon the cold germs won't catch up with you either!

There is no doubt that the ramp is part of our mountain culture. Its reputation has been ramped up and I suppose that it has now ascended an inclined plane to a favored place in our modern healthy eating pyramid.

PART IV

MORE MOUNTAIN LIFE

22

THE DAY THE THRESHERS CAME

THE WHEAT FIELD had turned from the green of the growing season to a golden color as the wheat ripened.

Grandad Rogers retrieved the cradle from the barn where it had been stored since this time last year. This was not the cradle that was used to rock a baby to sleep. This cradle was used to cut the stalks of wheat and gather the wheat after each time the cradle was swung through the standing wheat. There was a blade almost 3 feet long with a rack behind it to catch the wheat.

The cradle had a long handle and it was heavy. One stroke at a time taking down perhaps two feet of wheat stalks with each swing left a stubble a few inches from the ground. It took a lot of stamina and many strokes with the cradle to harvest a large field of wheat.

Grandad kept a file in his hip pocket and he would stop from time to time to sharpen the blade. A dull blade would make the cutting task even more difficult. A sharp edge on the blade was a necessity.

Someone must follow the man with the cradle to gather the wheat stalks into bundles with the golden grains of wheat at the end of each stalk. The bundles, or sheaves, were tied and stacked into structures called shocks, which were left standing in the wheat field until the threshers came.

Some may remember a song in the old Methodist Hymn-book called "Bringing In The Sheaves." Now you know what the songwriter was referring to.

Threshing day was a big event. There must be preparations, such as gathering all of the shocks of wheat and hauling them on a horse-drawn wagon to the site of the threshing.

The threshing machine was large and heavy and took a crew to operate. The sheaves of wheat were fed into the machine which separated the grains of wheat from the chaff and the straw. The straw was hauled to the barn to be used as bedding for the animals.

In pioneer days, the straw was put into heavy cloth bags and used as bedding, or mattresses, by our sturdy ancestors. Of course, feather beds were preferred but harder to come by.

Threshing time came during the heat of summer and was a hot and sweaty job. However, today the harvesting of wheat is much easier with much improved heavy machinery.

The men that came to my grandparents' farm on threshing day had to be fed. Tables for food were set up under the maple shade trees in the front yard of the farm house. There was a table in the backyard with buckets of water where the men could wash the dust and chaff from their arms and sweaty faces before being seated for a hearty dinner.

Grandmother, along with helpful neighbor women, would put a delicious meal before these hard-working men. They would move from farm to farm until all of the wheat in Crabtree community had been threshed and the grain had been stored in heavy sacks waiting to be carried to the grist mill as flour was needed in the kitchen at the farm house.

Threshing day was a bit similar to Hog Killing day, or maybe even a barn raising. It was a cooperative effort with many strong backs and willing hands needed. In those days, neighbors had to be real neighbors to make the culture operate successfully and not just neighbors in name only.

Threshing day did not put biscuits on the table (see the story titled "Piping Hot Whole Wheat Biscuits" in *Depression Baby*). There was other work to be done.

The sacks of grain had to be taken to the grist mill, the chaff had to be sifted from the flour and a skilled cook had to know how much baking powder or buttermilk to add to the mixture before a pan of biscuit dough was shoved into the oven. And oh yes, a rolling pin was needed to roll out the big lump of biscuit dough before the biscuit cutter did its job.

In grandad Roger's day preparing the soil to sow the wheat field was just the beginning of a process which involved threshing day, a grist mill, and a skilled cook to put biscuits on the table with sourwood honey or real sorghum syrup.

Today, when we reach into the frozen food cabinet for a package of biscuits at the local grocery store, let us remember and appreciate the multiple skills and the hard work of our ancestors and the knowledge they accumulated. Threshing day was important, but it was only a part of the farming process that I witnessed as a ten-year-old boy down on the farm.

23

UNPAINTED HOUSES AND TIRE ART

BACK IN THE 1930s and 1940s, there were many upainted houses scattered around our Southland. There was an abundance of durable lumber available like heart of pine, chestnut, or cypress that would last about forever without painting.

So why bother? There were more important things to do anyway, like going fishing.

Granddad John Burnett Medford built several small unpainted houses on Hanging Dog and some on Hall Top Road. These were rental houses and some were built of wormy chestnut, which is super expensive today.

The chestnut blight killed these beautiful trees. Huge skeletons turned a whitish silver as soon as the bark sloughed off of the giants. They were the largest trees growing in our Southern forests, and could be viewed high in the mountains where the logging companies could not get to them.

The ecology of the area was tremendously affected by the loss of a major wildlife food source, the chestnut. This lumber was plentiful and cheap, and few realized how much its value would increase.

My wife Lucy's mother Bertha Prisock Bradford lived in an unpainted house with a dog trot, before moving into fancier digs. The unique dog trot feature was common then.

The house was built in two sections with a breezeway connecting them. The dogs could get out of inclement weather in this covered area, and trot through with impunity.

A lot of houses didn't have grass lawns back in the "Dirty Thirties." They had dirt yards which had to be swept when company was coming. The homemade yard brooms were actually a bunch of broom sage tied on a stick...but it worked.

At least you didn't have to mow it with a reel push mower, which had to be sharpened frequently. Mowing with those buggers was not an easy task.

The dirt yards were well packed by the hound dogs and barefoot children, and they didn't look too bad when swept clean.

Whether painted or not, most respectable houses had flower pots on the porch, which were the pride and joy of the lady of the house. Begonias and geraniums were popular choices for porches while hen and chickens (a plant) quite often were in evidence. Hollyhocks and running roses adorned a lot of houses, with snowball bushes also being a favorite.

But more was needed to complete the picture. I call it tire art. A few worn out car tires placed strategically about the yard with some zinnias or petunias flowering in them were pretty cool.

The tires even looked better with some white paint on them, or maybe cut in a sawtooth design. Tires could also be cut in half and placed end to end for a real neat border. The ends were buried in the soil so that the tires wouldn't fall over. I've seen pictures of the Loch Ness monster with a similar visual effect.

We may not see many unpainted houses with dirt yards and outstanding tire art these days, for this was a transitional phenomenon as we moved from log cabins to our painted houses with their beautiful manicured lawns.

24

SIXTEEN TONS

SOMETIMES A SONG CAN BETTER EXPRESS an economic condition or the status of mankind than just the written word. *Sixteen Tons*, written by Merle Travis, may be one of those songs.

Tennessee Ernie Ford's booming bass voice told a story of a strong man who worked hard and...

> *I loaded sixteen tons of number nine coal*
> *And the straw boss said "Well, a-bless my soul"*
> *You load sixteen tons, what do you get?*
> *Another day older and deeper in debt*

This tale of woe was not unusual to the many poor people who lived in company villages or mill towns. The last line of the song brings to us the helplessness of the poor souls.

> *Saint Peter don't you call me 'cause I can't go*
> *I owe my soul to the company store*

And why does he say this? The mill or mine owners had

crafted a clever business plan with some attractive inducements, that went something like this: Come work in my mill and you can live in one of our little houses, constructed just for you and your family.

The house is really better than the house that you occupy as a tenant farmer. You can walk to work at the mill. (Most workers in that time frame did not own automobiles, so this was good.)

We have two churches, a Baptist and a Methodist, that are convenient for you to attend. You or your son might play on our baseball team, if you can play good enough. We have a schedule whereas we play against other mill town teams. We have a basketball schedule as well.

These workers were happy to get a job with all of these benefits, so they signed on and when payday came around, they received script. What is script, you ask? Not US dollars? Where can I spend this script? Why, the company store can supply all of your needs, and you can pay for all of this with the script.

Well, a-bless my soul.

You discover that the prices are higher in the company store than the stores over in town. Well, that's tough, man—take it or leave it. We are in a depression and jobs are scarce, and some people are going hungry.

This clever scheme, or we call it a business plan today, went on for many years. Cheaper labor brought the textile mills south from New England. Earlier, the textile industry had moved from England.

Again, cheaper labor lured the textile industry from southern United States to Bangladesh, Indonesia, China and other countries where labor is cheap. To coin a phrase, one might say "what goes around, comes around."

The unions rescued Tennessee Ernie Ford from the low pay in the mines, and the company stores disappeared. Now, government bureaucrats tell us that dirty coal has caused floods, snow and ice storms, and that climate change may cause the seas to rise.

The debate rages on and politicians give us dire warnings. The middle class fades from our midst and maybe the grandson of Merle Travis will write another song about all of this. Meanwhile,

> *Saint Peter, don't call me 'cause I can't go*
> *I owe my soul to the company store!*

25
—————

THE CARE PACKAGES

DURING MY HIGH SCHOOL YEARS, our family attended The First Methodist Church of Waynesville. It was a relatively large church with an upscale congregation. Not everyone had a lot of money but they were generally better off than the average citizen in the area.

Dad was required to dress in coat and tie, usually a suit to fulfill the job responsibilities as a school principal. He, of course, wore these same clothes to attend church.

Mother didn't have a lot of nice clothes that she felt comfortable in wearing to church. She felt underdressed. Therefore, Willie Boone did not attend church regularly.

Mother also didn't have as much education as most of the attendees of First Methodist. She had to drop out of school early to attend to her younger siblings since her mother, Maggie, died young, at forty-eight.

Sometimes, from all the way back in the Great Depression years, Mother would receive a package in the mail from Aunt Eleanor, wife of her brother, Hugh. Aunt Eleanor had very nice clothes and sometimes she had a surplus.

Her husband had a good job with the city of Greensboro, N.C. Hugh Medford was an engineer and very well thought of in Greensboro. They named a street after him.

Dad's sister, Aunt Iva Willis, also sent clothes to mother occasionally. Mother needed these clothes and seemed glad to receive them. It was gracious and kind of Aunt Eleanor and Aunt Iva to think of Mother.

These boxes of clothes affected me differently, although I knew Mother needed them. This made me feel like we were receiving charity. To me, it was like these gifts of love were CARE packages.

This proud boy of the mountains did not want any sort of welfare. I came from stock that was self-sufficient who would rather do without than be on the dole in any way. I know that my Mother did without so that us children would have decent clothes to wear to school. This made me feel sad and hurtful.

Most of the family went to church with Dad, but Mother would usually stay home to prepare us a good dinner, which would be ready when the troops returned from church. This made me feel guilty, so I would usually stay home with Mother.

With five or six children at home, a lot of things would get out of place. I would spend a lot of this time just putting the house in order. I knew that this gave my hardworking Mother some relief and also held my guilt at bay.

I wanted so much for Mother's situation to improve. My prayers were answered. Our family finances improved gradually as we children left the household.

When there was only my little sister, Dale, left at home, Mother could dress better and Dad could even take her out dinner on occasion. She began to enjoy attending church and felt more at ease in her surroundings.

The rewards of a frugal life and hard work finally came to

Mother and she no longer needed the care packages. There is a God.

26

WE CLEARED A NEW GROUND!

MR. ROBERTS WAS an old farmer who always wore overalls and a felt hat when he visited us. His big red long-haired dog was always with him, and the dog had a distinctive air about him. It appeared that he had never been bathed. (There is a pun in the above if you can sniff it out).

Mr. Roberts had a tract of land that he was not farming. It had grown over for years with brush and small trees. He offered this tract for my dad's use if he would clear it of the growth. In pioneer days, this was called "clearing a new ground"—not an easy task.

My dad was a school teacher at that time, and in the summer he was not teaching school. But he never had a summer vacation, as there were six children to support and eight mouths to feed.

He was always working during the summers, sometimes raising a tobacco crop which was the dominant cash crop in the western North Carolina Mountains at that time. Dad decided that one of his summer projects would be planting and marketing a pumpkin crop.

At that time, I was a fifth or sixth grader and old enough to be expected to do some hard work, so Dad and I started clearing and burning brush and cutting some trees. We cleared enough ground to plant a sizable pumpkin patch.

We also planted some kershaws, which were somewhat like a pumpkin as far as flavor and cooking qualities, but with a neck like a gourd. They were a mottled light green color similar to some watermelons.

The soil of the new ground was rich, and soon a sizable crop of pumpkins and kershaws were ready for harvest. I remember Mr. Roberts' mule-drawn farm wagon leaving our pumpkin farm piled high with the colorful fruits of our labor. This made me proud, and helped me forget the blisters worn on my hands during the chopping and sawing of the trees and clearing the bushes from the new ground.

The pumpkin crop was hauled by truck to the farmers market in Asheville, North Carolina. My younger brother Mark went along with Dad and me for this marketing venture. We didn't sell all of our pumpkins at the market, so we returned home with quite a few of our orange and green friends.

My dad proved to be an entrepreneur at this juncture. He negotiated a deal with the lunchroom ladies at the Red Oak School to give his five children some free lunches in exchange for the raw ingredients of pumpkin pies. The Red Oak School kids never knew how lucky they were to get organically grown pumpkin pies.

I don't know if there were any free lunches offered by the government to school children at this time, but you could bet your bottom dollar that my dad and mother would have been too proud to have accepted any such freebies.

Pumpkins were not the only fresh produce that found their way to the school lunchroom. I remember getting on the school bus with a bushel basket mostly filled with surplus tomatoes from our garden.

I don't remember being embarrassed by this venture, since some of other kids from time to time did likewise with all sorts of fresh, organically grown vegetables.

Of course, in today's government schools, with myriad regulations emanating from Washington D.C., this probably wouldn't be possible. But the lifestyles of the Depression era helped us to survive without going hungry—if one could endure things like growing a big garden, or maybe "clearing a new ground."

27

MUSIC IN THE MOUNTAINS

THEY CAME from England and from the Scottish Highlands and the cottages of Ireland, and they brought their music with them. Music was embedded in the genes of some families where almost everyone in the family played an instrument or sang.

There were the dulcimers resting on the laps of balladeers who sang of the homelands they had left behind. There were the fiddlers who brought alive the rhythms that made anyone with a drop of Irish blood spring to their feet and dance a lively jig.

The exuberance of the moment would bring my grandfather John Burnett Medford from dancing a jig to dancing like the russian Cossacks. Where he learned this, I will never know. The athletic abilities that enabled him to do this were amazing, as he performed at the Farmers Federation Annual Picnics.

As a week of following a plow horse or planting or harvesting a crop drew to a close, and the drudgery of it all built up in the veins of the farmers and their wives and children, Saturdays were a welcome occasion. Water was heated on kitchen stoves, and baths conducted with the aid of galvanized tubs, without the luxury of beautifully tiled showers that we now have.

The Saturday ritual still brought a cleansing effect to the body and soul as the anticipation of a Saturday night dance advanced to reality. A neighbor would remove the furniture from the largest room in the house for dancing. Or maybe my grandfather John Burnett would clear space in the country store run by his wife Maggie.

Wherever space was available, musicians would gather and the fun would begin. The strings of banjos would sing the songs in their own unique manner, and John Burnett's daughter, Willie Boone, would play a banjo with enthusiasm and skill. She might even bring her harmonica to play a background melody with a singer.

As the night progressed, someone might ask a friend to join him out beside the horse-drawn wagon that brought the family to the celebration. Surprisingly, there would be a jug or bottle hidden in the wagon.

The clear liquid contents of the jug had many names besides corn liquor, like "snake bite medicine" or "corn squeezin's" or moonshine, or maybe "mountain dew." After sharing refreshments a couple of times, the music seemed to go a little faster and a solo hoe-down might ensue.

When I was a teenager in Waynesville, there were Saturday night square dances at the Armory. Sam Queen called the dances, and he had his own dance team, which danced for the Queen of England on the occasion of her visit to the U.S.A.

Big Band music had become popular with many younger people in the forties and there were many fans of Tommy Dorsey, Jimmy Dorsey and Glenn Miller-type bands. The jitterbug dance came into vogue during World War II and young people loved this dance, which was featured in many movies. I played trombone in the fourteen-piece Teddy Martin band, who played dances in Western North Carolina and Eastern Tennessee.

My brother Mark and my brother-in-law Aaron Hyatt also played saxophone in the Teddy Martin band. The similar name caused the Teddy Martin Band to be confused with the nationally known Freddy Martin band. One couple told us they had traveled 400 miles to hear Freddy Martin...but they were good sports regarding the mixup.

We called traditional ballroom dancing round dancing. *All* dancing, except square dancing, we labeled as round dancing. When the question came up regarding attendance of an announced dance, the question was often asked "square or round?" A lot of the younger crowd tended to move toward round dancing during the forties, but they didn't entirely abandon the traditional square dancing.

The tourists who currently visit Maggie Valley in the summertime can still visit the Stomping Grounds Dance Hall to see the locals square dance and clog. The more adventurous visitors can join in the new experience of square dancing, and enjoy a dance that has been handed down through many generations of mountaineers.

The little family-oriented bands have morphed into nationally famous bands and individuals who perform at the pinnacle of country music in Nashville, at the Grand Ole Opry. And so, the legacy of our mountain music is not dead, and its offspring, bluegrass music, lives as a favorite of multitudes country wide. (Who doesn't love a lively rendition of "Rocky Top?")

The songs of Hank Williams and Roy Acuff (his rendition of "The Great Speckled Bird" was Mother's favorite) become sweet memories in the hearts and minds of those of us who grew up in the Great Smoky Mountains during the Great Depression and World War II. Music in the mountains has come a long way and is likely to thrive as an art form cherished by millions.

28

THE HAYWOOD COUNTY FAIR

COUNTY FAIRS and state fairs were a significant factor in rural America back in the early part of the past century. In the 1930s and 1940s there was no television and very little radio in some places, so entertainment and social functions such as county fairs were anxiously anticipated. The Haywood County Fair was held at the Band Mill Bottoms, but that is another story.

The farmers brought their prize livestock to the fair to be judged, and a blue ribbon for the best of breed was something to be proud of and shown to one's neighbors, and later displayed in the winner's home.

Peopled depended on animals in that era, and the animals depended on people. The mistreatment of animals that is an endemic part of the factory farms of today would not have been tolerated. Animals were allowed to be more closely in tune with nature, as God surely intended. The great sin of our time may well be the adverse treatment of our farm animals by the corporate farm structure subsidized by our Federal government.

A good Jersey or Guernsey milk cow was a prized and necessary possession, not only for farmers but for a lot of families living on the perimeters of the towns and cities. These breeds gave much richer milk than the Holsteins that provide most of our milk today. Rich cream was highly valued, and real whipped cream topped many desserts of the day. My grandfathers referred to milk without a lot of cream as "ole blue John" milk.

Teenagers brought their mature 4-H Club calves to be judged and later sold to the highest bidder, a sad day for these young people who had made pets of their calves. They curried and brushed their animals and fed them their favorite food, and then said their goodbyes. This was the end of the episode that their parents and teachers had prepared them for. An episode to be treasured and looked back on with fondness.

However, the parting of the 4-H calves from their owners may have been more than offset by the carnivals that came with the county fair. Everybody enjoyed he big ferris wheel, and the little ones thrilled to the music and the ride on the merry-go-round. This may seem tame to those who ride the scream machine rollercoasters of today, and I suppose it was.

The carnival brought the side shows, with maybe the "Fattest Woman Alive," or the "Alligator Man" or the "Smallest Man in the World," and the hoochie coochie tent that was for adults only. Young boys tried to get a peek, which would give them bragging rights for a week or so. The carnival might bring a gypsy fortune teller. A real gypsy tweaked the curiosity of this homogeneous mountain society.

The older boys would get to throw baseballs at some wooden bottles, and if they knocked down enough of them, they could win a stuffed animal for their girlfriends. Those who were not quite so energetic could toss rings over pegs to win—guess what?—more stuffed animals, or maybe a doll.

At the county fair, people strolled about from one event to another taking in the carnival atmosphere. Small children would enjoy the cotton candy, and there were the smells ranging from hamburgers cooking on open grills to other smells drifting from the animal barns. People might even visit the displays of prize fruits and vegetables, to see who got the blue ribbons and who had to settle for a red or yellow ribbon. Vegetables and fruits canned in glass Mason jars were also proudly displayed.

Ribbons were awarded for the best-looking babies. My twin brother and sister Mark Twain and Mary Jane won blue ribbons for the prettiest babies.

A few years later, my youngest sister, Dale, won the blue ribbon at the Red Oak School Festival for "Prettiest Baby," carrying on the family tradition. I suppose the family genes failed me when it was my turn to be judged, since the only blue ribbon I ever received was a Pabst Blue Ribbon. My only comment is that life ain't always fair. (Pun intended.)

The Cherokee Indian Fair was also held each fall in nearby Cherokee, with the unique feature of a game of roughly fought Indian ball. This fair was a regional event and was widely attended by the mountain people.

The Haywood County Fair, dinner on the grounds at the country churches, quilting bees, corn shuckings, and bluegrass music hoedowns in the living rooms of some mountain homes were some of the things that enriched the lives of our ancestors and were defining factors of our mountain culture.

29

BAND LIVES MATTER

IT WAS A BANNER DAY. Waynesville Township High School received a gift from the Gods. A young teacher, just out of college, came to our school to teach Band. His photo is in the 1943 school yearbook, *The Mountaineer*. This may have been the year that Waynesville was first blessed, but it could have been earlier.

This young man with the smile of a Hollywood star and an infectious laugh inspired all of his students. He certainly inspired me and made me want to excel. He wrote in my yearbook that I had made more progress that year than any of his students, but he didn't say how low down my standing was at the year's beginning.

Nevertheless, Charles Isley, Jr. became my favorite teacher. He inspired me to take my trombone to the North Carolina High School Band contests at Greensboro and come away with a Number One rating. Classmates Aaron Hyatt, Theresa Alley and Joe Morrow also received Number One ratings.

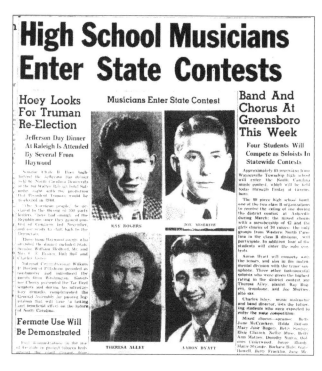

Courtesy Waynesville Mountaineer

Charlie also inspired my siblings. Jane and her flute, Mark with his great saxophone skills (he later had his own dance band at Western Carolina University, The Mark VI Combo), and Dale with her violin played in the school orchestra. Jane and Dale also performed with the school chorus. Charlie inspired my brother-in-law, Aaron Hyatt, to become a band director at Western Carolina University and later get a doctorate in music.

Charles Isley took over a music program that was in rags, literally. The band uniforms were just worn out. He organized an octet that sang barbershop and we sang for every civic club in Haywood County and everywhere else that we could to raise money for new uniforms.

With the new uniforms and the town establishment behind him, Charlie went on to mold a band that would be recognized as one of the three top bands in all of North Carolina—right up there with Charlotte Central High and Elizabethton High.

There was an event that is etched vividly in my mind. Charlie was determined to take the band to Charlotte for a parade, I believe. Apparently there were not funds in the band budget to charter a bus and maybe the school buses were not available, but Charlie was determined.

He drafted some old Army trucks originally designed to transport troops. For this trip, the troops were our band members. The trucks were covered with heavy canvas, but it was very cold and there was little comfort sitting on the wooden benches. Hey, but we were tough mountain teenagers and we made it without any frostbite.

When I got out of the truck and put my trombone together, I discovered ice in my spit valve. I looked across the parking lot as the Elizabethton band rolled up in their chartered, heated buses. The band students exited the buses in their warm woolen capes while we shivered in our new uniforms without top coats.

You see, the Elizabethton band was backed by a multi-millionaire who bought them anything they desired. They had practice rooms and the best instruments available, in addition to their capes and chartered buses. They were also a great band from a small town.

They *Waynesville Mountaineer* newspaper fully backed the Waynesville Township High School band with photos and articles about the band when we did well. The band was recognized in the yearbook and programs such as concerts. They didn't take a back seat to the sports teams.

And now, the rest of the story, as newsman Paul Harvey often said. Let us now fast forward to when my son, Bradford, enrolled as a freshman in the Lakeside High School band.

I proudly attended the first football game of the season and looked at the program brochure. The football team and coaching staff were featured in many prominent individual photos. The band had only one page of the brochure with a group photo so small that it was difficult to identify any of the band members. This is not the way that it was back in Waynesville, with the Charles Isley music department.

Lakeside High School had an outstanding football coach and a great team, and football was emphasized. Football was the thing. Maybe football players were idolized a bit too much, and some of the players became somewhat arrogant. I heard stories of some football players making fun of the band members. This I did not take lightly. In fact, I was pretty well ticked off.

Well, I decided to do something about the situation. I enlisted the cooperation of the band director, a photographer and a printer, and at the next football game and all subsequent ones, the band was featured as much as the football team. I was careful to keep what I was doing and my identity a secret.

Bradford and the other band members only knew that they were not looked down on at the school anymore, and that their efforts were recognized. I just hope that the band members held their heads a little higher and felt better about themselves.

Bradford moved on to later play tight end as a Lakeside Viking, and I have moved on, having learned from Charles Isley, Jr. that band lives matter.

PART V

FAMILY

30

MOTHER'S MYSTERY MAN

MOTHER WAS ONLY ABOUT SEVENTEEN, and he was maybe about nineteen, when they became girlfriend and boyfriend. This may have been her first real boyfriend. He probably grew up in the Iron Duff community where mother had always lived.

Maybe they came to know each other at the Davis Chapel Methodist Church where mother attended. Maybe they originally met in grammar school ...we will never know.

He wanted to see more of the world than this little mountain farming community, so he joined the U.S. Navy to "see the world," as was written on the Naval recruiting posters of that time. He began to widen his horizons as the Navy took him to many places, but he did not forget the pretty auburn haired girl that he left in the mountains.

He sent her a naval midi-shirt, which was a blue pullover, trimmed in white and part of his uniform. I can imagine that mother was impressed with this gift, for she had it cut down to her size. Perhaps she did the alterations herself, since at some point in her life she became a skilled seamstress.

Mother had a photograph made of herself in this part of a

Navy uniform and sent it to her boyfriend. I'm sure he showed the picture to his buddies, telling them that she was prettier than any girl they had met in any port.

And now the movie changes. Mother had a horse named Dan which she loved to ride. She and some of her friends rode their horses across Utah Mountain, where they came upon some other riders from the nearby Crabtree community.

Mother in her Navy midi-shirt.

My dad was one of those riders from Crabtree. They fell in love and subsequently married and had six children. The sailor man had been put aside. Maybe mother sent him a "Dear John" letter, but nevertheless he just became a memory to this busy little housewife and mother.

Time marches on as mother and dad lived a full life with children, grandchildren and then retirement for dad. Fate became a villain and our father was taken from us after 49 years of marriage to our mother.

Mother adjusted to her life as a widow, living in a little yellow cottage on Tate Street in Waynesville. She could walk to her First Methodist Church across the street and to her grocery store and to Main Street only a few blocks away.

Her sailor man may have been remembered from time to time, but mother had never heard from him. He had respected her marriage and had never tried to make contact with her...he was only a distant memory.

Not so with the sailor man, he never forgot mother. Maybe he married also and had children and grandchildren, but he apparently kept track of mother from a distance. He must have heard or read of dad's passing and pulled mother's photograph from his billfold once again to gaze at her image.

The respectful distance that he had always kept now became a narrow path as he saw Mother walking down Main Street. The sailor man mustered his courage and took this long walk across the street to approach a little lady who was in her seventies and who did not recognize him at first. He introduced himself for, after all, it had been over fifty years, and fifty years of living greatly changes everyone.

He told Mother that he had something to give her, and he slowly removed from his billfold the photograph that she had sent him long, long ago. He kissed it with his eyes one last time and handed it to mother, and with heavy heart departed.

Mother told us the story, but I do not know his name. Maybe he was married. We don't know, but they never reestablished a relationship. So the man who carried her photograph in his bill-fold for over fifty years must always remain mother's mystery man.

31

MAGGIE'S COUNTRY STORE

OVER 100 YEARS AGO, Maggie and her husband, John Burnett Medford, decided that the community of Iron Duff needed a store. They decided that Maggie would run the store and John Burnett would take care of the farm. I don't know if the frame building with a front porch was already in place, or if the building had to be constructed.

What was the shopping experience at Maggie's country store like? One can be assured that there was no resemblance to a trip that we might take to the mall, or to Macy's department store.

Maggie stocked the staples of the day, which included salt, sugar, coffee, flour, Calumet baking powder, and some canned goods. She may have had some Prince Albert tobacco in a can. The men rolled their own cigarettes from the cans of tobacco. Most women didn't smoke cigarettes, but a few older women smoked corn cob pipes.

The flour came in twenty-five- and fifty-pound bags. The bags came with colorful and attractive patterns, suitable for making dresses for the women and girls in the household.

Everyone at that time baked their own biscuits and cornbread. There were no sliced loaves of what we mountain people called light bread on the shelves.

There were no cars in Iron Duff at that time. Everyone depended on walking or horses for transportation, so Maggie probably stocked a few bridles and other items horsemen needed.

There could have been a few bolts of cloth suitable to making dresses for the women and young girls, and shirts for the menfolk. There were probably a few kegs of nails and axes, hammers, hoes, and shovels. There were no power tools.

There might have been a cracker barrel near the pot-bellied wood stove. A big hoop of cheese was probably on the wooden counter, with the scales nearby.

There probably was no cash register, but rather only a cash box. There wasn't a lot of cash around then, and barter was much in evidence. The farm wife didn't grab her credit card before going to Maggie's store, since credit cards hadn't been invented. Instead, she would take off her apron, put on a clean dress and send one of the children to the hen house to gather up some eggs.

The children were glad to oblige since they knew that the eggs could be bartered for something in Maggie's candy counter. Visions of red and white peppermint candy sticks or maybe a licorice stick would come to mind.

The farmer might load up a bag of freshly dug potatoes, or maybe a bushel of apples or tomatoes would be loaded into the wagon. Maybe a few chickens or ducks would be rounded up and put in a crate to be exchanged for the more expensive items like pots and pans.

Maggie had chicken houses and pens back behind the store to house the birds, waiting until enough accumulated to make it worthwhile for John Burnett to make a journey to Waynesville to sell the livestock to townspeople. Maggie's children would feed and water the chickens, and possibly ducks, geese and guinea hens. With six children in her family, Maggie could expect the older ones to help out with the store, as well as tending to the younger ones.

Maggie's children didn't expect an allowance. They saw how hard their mother and father had to work, so it just seemed natural to want to help out. It was just expected.

Maggie's son Hugh wasn't anxious to enroll in school at the customary age of five or six, and John Burnett and Maggie didn't push him. They let him just work in the store until he was eight, when he decided that he wanted to go to school. Maggie taught him to make change and perhaps how to read, just basic home-schooling.

Apparently, this late start did not damage Hugh academically. He graduated number one in his engineering class from North Carolina State University, and went on to become city manager of Greenville. A street there is named after him.

Maggie was an entrepreneur and started her own business in rural America, which was somewhat amazing. In that era, most women who worked outside the home were either school teachers or nurses. A few became secretaries.

Maggie obtained a book which cost $32.00, a high price for a book at the time. This book taught how to can and preserve foods. She taught a lot of women in the area these skills. She was sort of a county agent, without pay, and I am sure that a lot of families ate better food during the long winters as a result of her teaching.

I never knew my grandmother Maggie, because she died before I was born. But Maggie, I tip my hat to you. I am proud of all that you accomplished in your abbreviated life.

Your husband, John Burnett (he was always called by both names), was also proud of you. Years after your passing, he would show people the ledger book from Maggie's store, pointing out how neat and precise the book was. Maggie, you done good!

32

THE TERRE CORPORATION

AFTER GRANDFATHER JOHN BURNETT MEDFORD passed away in 1948, Mother and Dad purchased some land and at least a couple of Grandad's little rental houses.

One of the houses was perched at the crest of a high bank on Hall Top Road. The supports gave away and the house slid down the bank landing in a heap near the branch (creek) that ran through Hanging Dog. There was no insurance on this structure.

My father, Frank Lee Rogers, retired after a forty year career of teaching, and after being Principal of East Waynesville Elementary School for several years. The pinnacle of his tenure was being elected President of the North Carolina Educational Association.

The retirement income took care of their basic necessities but allowed little for luxuries, such as eating out occasionally. Mom and Dad loved to eat at the Lambuth Inn, located on a bluff overlooking beautiful Lake Junaluska, which is only a stone's throw from Waynesville, where they lived. There is a huge lighted cross near the entrance of the inn.

My siblings and I met to discuss our parents' dilemma. We all agreed that the real estate that our parents owned had appreciated some and was sure to appreciate more in the future. We were correct. A steakhouse is located where the Rogers homestead once stood. A big Publix Grocery Store occupies the area where brother Mark raised a tobacco crop in order to pay for his college education at North Carolina State University.

An oil company had shown some interest in the land in order to construct a service station. Mother and Dad needed additional income now, and the sale of the property logically should come later after the value had increased.

Our parents were proud people, and us children could offer some financial assistance. Each of our families was at a different level in climbing the economic ladder. But offering cash might seem like a handout or charity, and diminish their dignity. We didn't want to do that.

Mom and Dad were ferociously independent and self-sufficient. I believe this is a mountain thing, just a part of our culture.

A possible solution to the problem came to me, and I presented it to my brother and sisters. We would establish a corporation and place the real estate owned by mother and father in the company with them owning all of the shares. We children could purchase shares as we could afford and according to our parents' needs. When the property would be sold, everyone could cash in their shares. All of us agreed to move forward with the plan.

We needed a name for the Corporation. My sister Jane's husband Aaron Hyatt offered the name of Terre Corporation. Terre translated from French to English as land, which was descriptive of our basic asset.

The company was established by a local law firm and we moved forward with the plan. Mom and Dad had a bit more cash in their jeans, and Mom could now afford some fancy jeans.

Terre Corporation moved along doing its assigned job, and the property was sold at an appropriate time. Everyone cashed in their shares and Mom and Dad proceeded to live out their lives in the little yellow cottage on Tate Street just behind their beloved First Methodist Church.

The old home place, the barn and the little houses were bulldozed as the commercial interests had their way. Hanging Dog exists only in our minds now, and the Terre Corporation became some papers stored somewhere in a filing cabinet.

33

THE TRANSFORMATION OF
HANGING DOG

My brother Mark once said, "Hanging Dog is more than a place, it is a state of mind." But Hanging Dog, the place, as we knew it, is dead and gone. It is no more.

Author Thomas Wolf wrote *You Can't Go Home Again* in 1934. This was true then and it is true today. When you go back to the place you once called home, it is never the same. It will have changed, and most of the people are no longer there.

The three-room shack where Mother brought me into this world has long been torn to the ground. (See "The Good Old Days," in *Depression Baby*.) The other little rental houses that I called "Grandpa Medford's retirement plan" are no more. There was no Social Security income back then, but Gramps (Mother called him "Poppa") dropped by each house and collected ten dollars a month to put food and Sourwood honey on the table.

Gone forever are the bear hunting dogs (Plott hounds and Airedales) that belonged to Dr. Nick Medford, my great-uncle. We can no longer hear their barking up on Frazier Street or an occasional howling at a full moon. Guess the black bears of our Smokies will be glad to hear of this.

The tobacco field where brother Mark raised a crop to earn money to pay his tuition at North Carolina State University is covered with an asphalt parking lot. (See "Justifiable Homicide" in *Depression Baby*.) I guess Mark learned down at State how to make sage observations like "Hanging Dog is a state of mind."

Hall Top Road is no more. The gravel road led up to Grandfather Medford's mountain place where his milk cows were pastured. Sister Sara used to walk up this road past the tenant houses to her summer job of waiting tables at the Hall Top Resort, where rich people from Florida spent their summers enjoying the cool mountain air in those days before air conditioning. The four-lane Waynesville Bypass cut off Hanging Dog from the mountain pasture, which is now covered in trees.

Our two-story frame house described in the story "Were They Angels?" has been replaced with a steakhouse. Actually, Mom's home cooking could surpass anything any steak house could offer, in my humble opinion.

The little branch (a small creek in Mountain talk) we used to play in, and where we gathered duck eggs for Mom to use in making tea cakes, is now enclosed in a culvert and covered with tons of dirt. The apple trees that I planted along this little stream no longer produce apples for Dad to proudly give away.

The little church where the poor people went to worship has been replaced with a new building housing an upscale Publix grocery store. We will never again hear the preacher shouting his warnings of hell and damnation. Publix will offer food for the body and the preacher has gone elsewhere to offer his food for the soul.

34

JOHN BURNETT'S LEGACY

GRANDAD JOHN BURNETT MEDFORD came through the back door of Mother's home, quietly greeting his daughter Willie.

"Hello, Poppa," Mother said. She always called him Poppa.

I believe that he was making an inspection tour, since Mother and Dad had just moved into the two-story frame home from a smaller house on Hanging Dog.

John Burnett (people used his double name in true Southern style) usually walked with both hands clasped behind his back as if in deep thought. Maybe he was thinking through some business deal. He owned considerable real estate, acquired by his keen business sense and bestowed unto his children as he felt their need.

Willie's Poppa strolled through the kitchen and into the dining room. He stopped in the empty room and turned to Mother.

"Willie, you don't even have a dining room set," he said.

"We can't afford to buy anything," Mother replied, exposing the reality brought on by a school teacher's meager salary. Dad taught school for forty years.

Saying nothing, John Burnett walked through the living room and out the front door. A couple of hours later, a furniture truck pulled up beside my parents' home and some men brought an oak dining table with six chairs into the house, along will a small serving table.

It was about ninety years ago that this badly needed gift arrived in Willie's household. She lovingly placed her wonderful food creations on this table while raising six children.

Dad asked the food to be blessed thousands of times, and we sat in the oaken chairs talking and laughing as the years slipped by. The wear and tear of six active children and their friends began to take its toll, as one by one the once solid chairs became rickety and were placed in the attic.

My brother Mark in his teenage zeal decided to clean out the attic. He tossed the stricken chairs into the yard and burned them. But one chair was saved. It had a purpose.

After Mom and Dad had passed and we siblings were dividing their belongings, none of them showed much interest in the table. It was indeed pretty shabby with the finish almost turned black. Brother Mark had also placed a board on the table to saw it—and saw it he did. He cut through the board and cut a nick in the table.

Years later, Lucy and I had just completed restoration of the Little White House in the Noxubee Wildlife Refugee. We took the dining furniture and Dad's bookcase, also in bad shape, to Mississippi. When my teenage stepson Derrick saw what I had brought to our newly finished house, he took Lucy aside and said to his Mom, "You've got to stop Ray from bringing this crap down here. He is going to ruin this place."

A Mennonite gentleman had installed our kitchen cabinets and had done a good job. He referred us to his nephew, Kevin Yoder, and told us that he would do us an excellent job restoring our old furniture.

And so he did! Kevin was a real craftsman making everything better than new. He went one step further. He took the one remaining chair that had escaped brother Mark's wrath and used it as a pattern to make five exact copies. (Just kidding, Mark).

We were indeed fortunate. The oak table and chairs add distinction to our restored farmhouse and fit perfectly. Not to worry, Derrick.

Mother must be proud to know that Poppa's legacy and kindness lives on. Thank you, John Burnett.

35

TEACHING IS IN OUR GENES

THERE IS no doubt that teaching is in our genes, since so many of our clan have been in the education or teaching profession. Let's start with Asbury Thornton Rogers, who was a teacher in addition to being a farmer and an officer (Captain) in the Confederate Army.

Esther Lorena Davis Rogers, wife of Asbury, was known as the "teaching" grandmother by the children of John and Mary Elizabeth Rogers, since she always brought a spelling or reading book when she visited her grandchildren.

The grandmother from the Hipps-Cody side of the family was known as the "fun" grandmother because she would get down on the floor and play with her grandchildren. However, her teaching was a bit different. She taught the little ones songs and games. Our Dad learned "Hebo, hibo, hey, hey, hey" (a family song) from this grandmother.

It would seem that the children of Asbury and Lorena got a double shot of teaching genes. John Rogers, the eldest son of Asbury and Lorena, had to quit school early due to family responsibilities, since his father died when he was only age thirteen. However, John had great respect for education and several of his children went to college, which was not common in that era.

The schools in Haywood County were consolidated and the children who lived on Crabtree Creek would have to be bused to a distant school— but the school board decided that they didn't have enough money to furnish a bus for the kids on Crabtree Creek.

John Rogers would have none of this. He probably had to sell some cattle to raise the money, but he bought a bus with his own money and told the school board that they could pay him back when they got the money...and the children of Crabtree Creek got to continue their education.

Margaret "Maggie" Medford, wife of John Burnett Medford, my grandfather, was not a teacher in the usual sense. However, she made a big contribution to her community in another way. Maggie purchased a very expensive book for that time for over thirty dollars. She used this book to teach the women who lived in the Iron Duff Community how to cook and can and preserve food for their families. She probably passed her knowledge to the ladies in an informal manner when they came to her country store to shop. Yes, Maggie ran a store in addition to raising a family.

My great Uncle Clark Medford was a writer who produced six or seven books, mostly historical. He also wrote a column in the *Waynesville Mountaineer* and the *Asheville Citizen* newspapers titled "Uncle Abe," since his physical features resembled Abraham Lincoln. Clark also taught school for part of his life.

Great Aunt Elizabeth "Lizzie" Rogers, daughter of Asbury Thornton Rogers, became principal of Robinson Elementary School in Gastonia. Very few women held the title of principal at this time.

Another exceptional person, Stewart Cramer, owner of

Cramerton Mills, wanted the children of his mill workers to get a good education. He enticed Aunt Lizzie to resign her position as school principal and come to the school he provided for his mill workers, to teach the third grade. He paid her more than she was making as a principal.

John Rogers was a self-educated man, well respected in his community. Some of his neighbors and friends tried to convince him to run for the state legislature, but he refused, preferring to continue his farming and raising his fourteen children. His love of education, although denied to him, was reflected in ten of his offspring teaching for at least a portion of their lives.

My father Frank Lee Rogers led the charge by teaching for forty years, many of them as principal of the East Waynesville Elementary School. He was also honored to be elected as President of the North Carolina Teachers Association.

Aunt Esther taught for the Gaston County school system. Aunt Lizzie had brought her down to Gastonia to teach in her school. Aunt Esther put her roots down there and married Uncle Steve and raised her family in Gastonia. Uncle Hugh was principal of Cruso Elementary in Haywood County. Aunt Lorena taught at the Crabtree School where her husband, Charles Duckett, was principal. Aunt Iva taught in the Asheville school system. Aunt Elizabeth (Libby) taught in Jacksonville, Florida.

Uncle Zebulon Vance (Zeb) Rogers taught in South Boston, Virginia. Uncle Zeb's daughter, Rosalind Rogers Vellines, taught in Richmond, Virginia for several years when she was just out of school. Her sister, Caroline Rogers Lacy, taught for one year in Germany at a school provided for servicemen, while her husband served in the military there.

Uncle John Rogers taught electronics at North Carolina State University. Aunt Helen taught with Aunt Lizzie in Gastonia. Aunt Clara taught in Canton. Wow, what a family of teachers!

Cousin June Stowe taught at Salisbury, and her brother

Roger Stowe served for eight years on the Gaston County School Board. My sister Jane Hyatt taught as head of the Interior Design Department at Western Carolina University. Jane's husband, Dr. Aaron Hyatt had an outstanding career in education, including teaching music and serving as Dean of Graduate School at Western Carolina University. Aaron later became President of Macon College in Georgia for twelve years. Aaron brought the college from a two-year school to become Macon University, quite an accomplishment.

Jane and Aaron's daughter, Sharyn Hyatt-Wade, received the Teacher of the Year award in the field of art for the entire state of Missouri. Sharyn and Dale Wade's son Sawyer is in his first year of teaching graphic arts. He must be well-liked for all of his students to have him featured on their cell phones.

Peggy McCracken, daughter of Aunt Myrtle Medford McCracken, was a teacher of music in Haywood County. Two sons of Elizabeth "Libby" Rogers Rutledge were teachers early in their lives. Gary Rutledge taught for one year before going to law school, and Ronnie taught in Jacksonville, Florida for seven years before beginning his career in social services.

Rachael Duckett Jones, granddaughter of Lorena Rogers Duckett, is currently teaching at Jonathan school near Maggie Valley. Terry Rogers, great grandson of Asbury, taught two years at Haywood Technical Institute, now Haywood Community College.

Eula Adeline Rogers Belich, granddaughter of Asbury Thornton Rogers, taught at Crabtree School. Adeline's granddaughter Rebecca Gunther taught school in Kentucky. Adeline's sister, Eva Jane Rogers Tate, taught in Haywood County, in the state of Washington and in New England. Eva Jane's daughter Judy Tate taught in Henderson, North Carolina. Eva Jane's granddaughter Taylor Mancuso is currently teaching.

Great granddaughters of Asbury and daughters of Edwin

Rogers, Margaret Rogers Bowers taught at Canton, North Carolina, and Kathey Rogers Beach taught at Virginia Beach. Hazel Rogers Chapmen, granddaughter of Asbury taught at Beaverdam, North Carolina.

That brings us to Dr. Gene Ford, who sang with the Metropolitan Opera for many years. Cousin Gene has sung for four U.S. Presidents as well as the Pope. Dr. Gene has been an outstanding teacher in his chosen field of music.

My own son, Bradford Rogers, currently teaches folks around the world how to produce music, edit video, and much more via his popular show *The Multimedia Ninja*.

Well, I guess that teaching must be in our DNA to produce this many educators in our extended family. I hope I haven't left out anyone. Oh yes, I must include my own contribution to the field of education. I was appointed as class librarian of the third grade at Cullowhee Elementary School. Teacher's pet! Hey, I even had my own special little desk. Awesome!

PART VI

FROM HANGING DOG TO JUPITER

36

OKIES FOR A DAY

THE DEPARTMENT OF EDUCATION of North Carolina had spoken, and Frank L. Rogers got the message.

If Frank wanted to continue as a teacher in North Carolina, he must have a four year college degree. My teacher in the first and second grade in 1935 and 1936 only had a high school education, but this would no longer be allowed. Dad must go back to college.

But here was the dilemma: Dad had five children and a wife to provide for, and practically no savings. There were no relatives that could "send" him to school and no student loan programs. With great courage and faith, a decision was made. They would bite the bullet and "git 'er done."

They rented a large two story frame house, and they found a pasture and a barn up the road a piece to house the family milk cow. Now all that they had to do was find some boarders to fill the house to provide income while Dad was in school. Living in a boarding house with meals provided was not unusual during the Great Depression.

The Western Carolina Teachers College was within walking

distance of Mom and Dad's newly-acquired big yellow house, and several college students signed onto the plan. All Mother had to do was cook for seven family members and about eight boarders. Not a small order for this petite little lady of unbounded tenacity. All that I can say is that Dad picked a winner.

(One boarder was Dad's younger brother, Hugh, and another was his youngest sister, Libby.)

Now, the next step in this saga. The furniture, livestock and children must be moved from the community of Iron Duff in Haywood County to the community of Cullowhee in Jackson County.

My parents couldn't afford to engage the services of professional movers such as Mayflower or North American with their enclosed moving vans. The U-Haul concept of moving hadn't even been thought of. The nearest comparison of a moving concept today would be the Two Men and a Truck company, but this organization was years away from offering their services.

Well, Frank probably found someone with a pickup truck with high railings installed to transport the cow to her new environment.

As I remember, two stake body trucks with high beds were found whose owners sometimes moved people locally. But there were two big problems: No covered truck beds and no tarps.

Now is the time that one must visualize. In this same time frame, the farmers in Texas, Kansas, Oklahoma and other states were enduring drought and dust storms. The topsoil was literally being blown away from their farms.

The suspended dust in the air resulted in brilliant sunsets even as far away as Western North Carolina. This is just about the only positive in this drama.

John Steinbeck wrote of the suffering of these people living in the Great Plains, and their journeys to the West. Henry Fonda did a superb job of acting in the movie version of Steinbeck's *The Grapes of Wrath.*

Everything that these victims of nature's wrath owned was loaded onto open bed trucks for all the world to see, as they headed West for a new start in California.

The Rogers family did something very similar, as we headed for new opportunity in the shadow of what is now Western North Carolina University. We had faith in what the education of our Father would bring us.

Half of our family was in the cab of each truck with the drivers. Dad's brother Uncle Hugh, and another school teacher as well, came to help out with our migration. There was not room for Hugh in the truck cabs, so he rode in the back of one of the trucks—along with a cage or two of chickens, which were piled high with various household goods.

The Okies were on the move.

During our journey, the family cat escaped from its place of confinement. To prevent the cat from jumping off of the truck, Uncle Hugh caught the cat and placed it in one of the chicken coops with a bunch of pecking hens.

When we arrived at our destination, the cat was let out of his torturous place of confinement. Well, kitty cat got the "hell out of Dodge" and was never seen again. Can you blame him?

To add to the misery of it all, the heavens opened up to release a copious amount of rain. With no defense provided, everything the Okies from the mountains owned was soaked.

Because of the muddy situation, the trucks could not back in close to the porch, so the men had to carry the furniture down a red clay bank. I suppose that it could be aptly said that "when it rains, it pours." (Courtesy of Morton Salt.)

Another moving story needs to be added at this point. The Rogers family moved again at a later date from the community of Jupiter. (Yep, that's right...Jupiter. Far out, right?)

We were well on our way to our home in Waynesville, N.C. when one of the drivers saw in his rearview mirror a neighbor lady waving frantically and running up the road with my sister, Jane, close behind.

It seems that Jane was almost left behind in Jupiter. Moving day apparently is not a good time for cats and little sisters.

The Rogers family survived our Okie-like moves and the boarding house adventure. Dad got his diploma and the Department of Education was happy.

To top it off, all of us were filled with pride when Frank L. Rogers was elected President of the North Carolina Education Association, a rather high achievement for an Okie from the Smokies.

37

FROGGY WENT A-COURTIN'

FRIENDS, Romans and countrymen, lend me your ears—or at least your eyes—and allow me to set the stage.

The time was about 1938 and the Frank Lee and Willie Boone Rogers family were firmly settled in a community called Jupiter. (Far out, huh?) A barn and a cow pasture and a garden site came with our rented house.

Dad taught at Red Oak School and his teacher's contract did not allow any alcohol or even playing cards in our house. At that time, teachers were to be role models for their students and their conduct was expected to be impeccable. The culture of our current time would quite likely label this as dullsville, or worse.

TV had not been invented and radio often came with a lot of static. The concept of cell phones and texting had probably never entered the human mind. Birds, not people, twittered.

As you can imagine, entertainment was a scarce commodity. The Gilbert and Sullivan comic opera *The Pirates of Penzance* that we performed at our school was a welcome diversion. We were not totally culturally deprived as we mountaineers may have been perceived elsewhere.

Now enter at stage left our Uncle Hugh Rogers, armed with his guitar and his harmonica, to furnish us with songs and copious humor.

There was a device that fitted on his neck that allowed him to play the guitar and harmonica at the same time. Kind of a one man band.

We loved Hugh's little songs and to us he was a troubadour. He brought us live entertainment that filled a void as we sang and laughed with him. Good ole Uncle Hugh!

One song still sticks in my memory after all of these years. The song was on old Scotch ballad handed down to us through singers such as Uncle Hugh for four hundred years or so, with the unlikely title of *Froggy Went A-Courtin'*.

The words and verses were altered over the years as they were handed down through the memories of many singers. But this didn't matter, as children used their imaginations to create whatever they wanted Froggy or Miss Mousie to be.

Singer Bob Dylan recorded his version of this little song that went something like this (pat your foot and play your air guitar... here we go!):

> *Froggy went a-courtin' and he did ride, uh-huh*
> *Froggy went a-courtin' and he did ride, uh-huh*
> *Sword and pistol by his side uh-huh*

> *He rode right up to Miss Mousie's door, uh-huh*
> *He rode right up to Miss Mousie's door, uh-huh*
> *Saw Miss Mousie a sittin' on the floor, uh-huh*

> *He took Miss Mousie on his knee, uh-huh*
> *He took Miss Mousie on his knee, uh-huh*
> *Said* Miss Mousie, will you marry me? *uh-huh*

Many singers, including Elvis Presley, Woody Guthrie, Tex Ritter, Burl Ives and even Bruce Springsteen have recorded versions of this classic.

There are many additional verses. One version even has Froggie and Miss Mousie having children, but I will cut to the last verse:

A little piece of cornbread on a shelf, uh-huh
A little piece of cornbread on a shelf, uh-huh
If you want any more, you can sing it yourself, uh-huh

Friends, Romans and countrymen, you can play with this little ditty any way you like—but once you sing the tune, I warn you, it may stick in your head.

Well, we're through with Froggy, but Uncle Hugh deserves a bit more.

He served his community well as principal of Cruso School in Haywood County until his retirement. He was a trout fisherman par excellence.

Since my dad didn't fish, Hugh would take up the slack and bring our family a mess of mountain trout on occasion. To interpret our mountain talk, a *mess* of trout adequately fed our family, but could not be divided to feed the masses as in the Bible story.

While fishing with his girlfriend, as a young man, Hugh snagged his friend with a fish hook. He decided to get medical help to remove the hook and took her to the Haywood County Hospital for the procedure.

I cannot verify the truth here, but as the story goes, Hugh did not cut the fishing line, and he still had her on the line when he walked into the doctor's office. Well, why shorten a perfectly good spool of fishing line? I don't know what happened to the romance, but I doubt she ever fell for him hook, line and sinker.

Again, thank you, Uncle Hugh, for bringing Froggy to us children, and the messes of trout that you most generously bestowed will never be forgotten.

38

SANTA COMES TO JUPITER

AT CHRISTMASTIME when I was young, we always put out a snack for Santa. Mom made freshly baked tea cakes that were placed on the table with a glass of milk. The milk and cookies (no store-bought stuff) were always gone the next morning, so there must have been a Santa.

One Christmas I asked Santa Claus for a tricycle. My older sister Sara may have written a letter to Santa for this little three-year-old. Sara looked out for us younger ones.

Sometime during the night, I awakened and decided to check to see if Santa had come. The light of the coals in the fire-place revealed to me that Santa had not forgotten this little mountain boy. This was one of the happiest moments of my life and was probably my first memory.

I couldn't wait for morning. I rode the little tricycle around and around the room by the light from our fireplace.

It was rare for any of us kids to get a toy as expensive as this trike. Of course, there were only three children in the family at that time and Santa did not have to divide gifts among six children as was necessary later on.

Usually, there was a chair for each child placed in a semi-circle in front of the fireplace. Santa placed some items of clothing in each chair and some oranges and a few pieces of candy in our stockings. That was about all Santa could afford.

When I was in the fourth or fifth grade, Santa brought me a toolkit scaled down to my size. (Another exception.) I put this gift to good use by building a little doll bed for my sister Jane out of some mahogany wood from a discarded sofa.

I had forgotten this event until Jane recently thanked me for building this toy bed. This brought back memories of making toy cars and trucks with my toolkit. I even built a little boat powered by a rubber band with a rudder that guided the boat around and around a large galvanized tub filled with water. We didn't have another water source at Jupiter.

When I was in the fourth grade, I was exploring the attic when I discovered Santa had hidden our gifts there. While in the first or second grade, I had already heard that our parents were really Santa. I believe my buddy James Chambers and I had a conversation regarding this possibility.

My younger brother and sister (Mark and Jane) were in the first grade at that time. I couldn't wait to show them what they were going to get from Santa. Jane remembers the pretty mirror and hairbrush.

Mark and Jane did not spill the beans about their newly acquired knowledge, and neither Jane nor I remember having any adverse effects from learning the truth about Santa. In fact, this only increased the admiration for my parents and the sacrifices they made to provide gifts from Santa. We continued to let our parents think that we believed in Santa for some time.

39

IT WAS A GAME CHANGER

WHEN DAD GOT his degree at Western Carolina Teachers College (now University of Western North Carolina), we moved to Jupiter, which was just a wide place in the road.

Our home was a two story frame house and we also had a tobacco barn. There were several large oaks surrounding the house, which had a cistern to collect rainwater. There was a kitchen sink with a hand pump at one end to bring water from the cistern into the kitchen. No city water here, but there was a large pump outside to bring water up from a well.

My brother and sister, twins Mark Twain and Mary Jane, would play with little vehicles that I manufactured just for us. I would cut a slice from an old broomstick, bore a hole in the center and, presto, I had a wheel. A heavy piece of wire served as an axle and soon we had a little wooden car. We had little roads around the base of the oak trees and even tunneled a road under one of the exposed roots.

Life was different in those days. We had never heard of a toy store. We would build forts, and gather buckets of acorns for ammunition to have acorn fights. The acorns didn't hurt much, even if you received a direct hit.

When I was a little older, I received aa a gift a kit to build a Piper Cub airplane. It was built from lightweight balsa wood and covered with light weight yellow paper with a rubber band to furnish power for the propeller. It was a beautiful little plane, and I wound up the device to take its maiden flight from the dining room into the living room. The family cat saw my little plane landing and she jumped on it and crushed it. This was the last plane I built.

My friends, E.B. and Jimmy Debrull, lived across the gravel road in a little modern log cabin. Their dad had a car (we had none) and commuted to his job in Asheville. He told us of an acrobatic show coming to Asheville. We talked him into taking us to see the show, which greatly impressed us.

When we returned to our country home, we decided to put on our own show in the tobacco barn. A tobacco barn has wooden poles going from one side of the barn to the other side, on which tobacco is hung to cure. The poles were bare of bark and perhaps a little slick.

Each of us guys would put on an act maybe 10 to 15 feet above the barn floor. Something went awry during my performance and down I came, striking a board leaning against the barn wall as I fell. My left arm was not only broken but was knocked out of socket at the elbow. As I ran to the house, my arm below the elbow was sticking out at a strange angle.

As we rushed to the hospital in Asheville for treatment, thoughts ran through my head that my arm would not ever be the same, and that my arm might be withered like a boy in our school whose arm just kind of hung by his side. I never told anyone of my fears, like I should have, so my fears stayed with me during recovery.

The orthopedic doctors in Asheville had a difficult time

getting my arm back in socket and setting the broken bone. My arm healed with a slight curvature. Its performance was adequate but it was never as strong as my right arm. At least my fears of a withered arm never materialized, thank God.

When I went out for spring football in high school, I did well in the eyes of the coaches because of my speed, but we just ran plays and did not get into heavy blocking and tackling. As the fall sign up for football neared, Dad and I had a discussion regarding the possibility of breaking my left arm again and what the results might be.

Dad never told me that I could not go out for football. I decided I would play basketball, which had much less risk, rather than football. It was a literal game changer. Some of my friends were football players, and I was kind of left behind and out of the same high school circles.

Later in life, I was called up for the draft during the Korean War. When I was examined, the doctor looked at my left arm closely and made some notes. I was turned down for service in the Army because of my arm, another game changer. I was never afraid of going into the Army, I was just looking at the possibility of another adventure.

Previously, near the end of World War II, the big one, me and three of my buddies decided that we would quit high school and join the Airforce. We all piled into a friend's car and were off to the recruiting office in Asheville. I wanted to fly one of those fighter airplanes and be a war hero. I say "airplane" because jets had not yet been invented. I failed the eye test and this was another game changer. The fact that I was never in the service may have saved my life.

So here I am folks, eighty-nine years old and writing a book about my life, because a couple of game changers actually changed my life.

40

ANY BONDS TODAY

THE FIRST FUNDRAISER that I remember was at the Red Oak School that I attended when we lived at Jupiter.

We had been attacked December 7, 1941 by Imperial Japan at Pearl Harbor by a large naval force. Zero airplanes, piloted by warriors who were willing to make suicidal dives into American war ships in service to their god-like emperor, sunk a large part of our Navy. The ghostly battleships still live at the bottom of the port in Hawaii.

Valiant Great Britain, led by Winston Churchill, had fought Hitler's blitzkrieg and had miraculously retreated from Dunkirk across the English channel to fight another day. France, Belgium and the Netherlands had fallen in defeat. Our backs were to the wall.

President Franklin Delano Roosevelt declared war on Hitler's Nazi hordes, Benito Mussolini's fascist Italy and Hirohito's Imperial Japanese forces, who would fight to the last man rather than surrender. Our enemies were called the Axis.

We were desperate. We must defeat the Axis, or western civilization as we know it would cease to exist.

Our boys volunteered by the thousands and became men immediately. The draft was set up to fill any void. The auto plants were shut down (no cars were built during World War II) and converted to build tanks and other military vehicles. The word "jeep" became a part of our vocabulary.

Shipyards turned out thousands of ships, only to see many go to the bottom of the sea as victims of the axis submarines. "Loose lips sink ships" posters were seen everywhere. We were trying to thwart any spies and save ships and lives. Letters to and from servicemen were censored.

Gasoline was rationed. Tires were rationed. Shoes were rationed, as well as sugar. But the bootleggers always seemed to find some. Ladies had no nylon stockings. Nylon was needed for parachutes

The war machine needed money. Lots of money , and the patriotic citizens of America responded. Kate Smith sang "God Bless America" with conviction and fervor. Her rendition made you want to stand up, put your hand over your heart and sing with her.

Citizens wanted to help our country, help us survive as a nation. Hollywood even pitched in, in a big way. Gene Autry sang a song in the movie *Home in Wyomin'* in 1942, "Any Bonds Today". The Andrews sisters, very popular singing group, also recorded "Any Bonds Today." The radios blared the words in homes across our nation.

Patriots flocked to bond rallies to buy war bonds. They sang "The Star-Spangled Banner" and listened to patriotic speeches. But more importantly, they opened up their wallets to lend money to our country. They wanted to give our servicemen the ultimate support.

Almost everyone had someone close to them in the Army, Navy, Air Force, Marines or Coast Guard. My dad had five brothers and one sister in the service during World War II.

Women joined the WACs, WAVEs, and SPARs. "Rosie the Riveter" made the women defense plant workers be appreciated for their efforts.

Little children brought their pennies, dimes and quarters to school to buy Defense Stamps to stick in little books. When the book was full of stamps (eighteen dollars and seventy-five cents), the smallest war bond could be purchased at a bond rally. Ten years later, it would be worth twenty-five dollars when cashed in.

Massive amounts of money were raised at these rallies toward the three hundred billion-dollar cost of the war to preserve our freedom. These bond rallies allowed everyone from the children to the very wealthy to do their part.

PART VII

FROM JUPITER TO MARS HILL

41

THE GREAT ALARM CLOCK CAPER

THE BUSY DAYS at Waynesville Township High School were coming to an end seemingly before I was ready to leave this life-style and step into another stage of life.

Some of my friends were talking excitedly about the colleges they planned to attend. One friend was agonizing about choosing between two schools that he might attend. I was unable to enter these conversations and I felt left out, a different form of agony.

My afternoons after school during my senior year were spent at the Winn Dixie grocery store. I had quit the varsity basketball team that I had played on as a starter my junior year. (We won the Western North Carolina conference. But that's another story.)

Mr. Ralph Summerow, who owned Ralph's Super Market in nearby Hazelwood, sought me out to manage his meat market and teach his brother Lawson how to be a butcher. Lawson had just recently gotten out of the U.S. Army and was eligible under the G.I. Bill to have his education paid for by Uncle Sam. Somehow, Ralph got me qualified as a teacher under the G.I. Bill and our plan moved forward.

We agreed that I would work at Ralph's grocery store for one year and an additional summer, in exchange for enough salary to extend my education a couple of years—providing that I lived with my parents and didn't buy a car.

I pretty much walked away from my friends from high school. I didn't fit in anymore. They were college rah rah and I was just an employee of a grocery store. But I knew I was headed in the right direction.

I looked for the cheapest college that I could find, and I got lucky. I matriculated at Mars Hill College, a little two-year Baptist school north of Asheville, North Carolina.

The teachers seemed to really care about this wayward student who hadn't studied a lot in high school. Mars Hill was virtually classless in that there were not fraternities or sororities there. The students were friendly and I soon had a large circle of friends.

I joined the band, along with my trusty trombone, and was Drum Major for a while. I made the track team running the hurdles and only lost one race my second year on the team, when I let the Davidson College guy beat me by one pace. I even joined the boxing team for a spell. Life was good.

Mars Hill was the school of choice for a lot of students who planned to become Baptist ministers. We had chapel services about twice a week, with Dean Lee presiding. Needless to say, these sessions were not tremendously exciting and hardly a good fit for the exuberance of some of us. So one day, a closely knit group of friends decided to enliven the chapel meeting.

Chapel was held in a former church building. The windows were high and had drapes to the side of each window. A plot was hatched: We would gather a number of alarm clocks and set them so they would go off a few minutes apart.

Chapel had begun and Dean Lee was droning on and on when the first alarm went off. There was a mad scramble to find a ladder to quiet the alarm clock cleverly hidden behind the drapes.

Order was restored and Dean Lee cranked it up again, but another alarm clock started up on the other side of the auditorium. The pandemonium increased as other alarms tested the religion of even the most devout.

Dire threats were issued regarding the future of the guilty ones. The mystery could have been easily solved by inspecting the dorm rooms to see who did not have an alarm clock. I must confess that I had to replace my Baby Ben alarm clock. Yes, Dean Lee, I was guilty as sin.

42

DID MARS HILL COLLEGE BOYS WEAR LIPSTICK?

MARS HILL COLLEGE is a Baptist school nestled in the mountains North of Asheville, North Carolina. It was the perfect place to send your daughter to college back in the fifties and be confident that she would be protected from carousing and decadent college boys.

To be certain, the parents noted that the girls' dorms were located on a hill that was separated from the boys' dorms by the main campus.

The girls' dorms were well monitored by house mothers, who lived on the first floor of the dorm. Boys could not proceed beyond the lobby area of the girls' dorm and girls could not enter the boys' dorms, period. To do so would probably have meant that the girl would have been expelled and promptly sent home to her parents.

If a female coed wanted to go shopping in the nearby city of Asheville, she must have written permission from her parents. Of course, the girls could not live off campus. However, boys could live off campus, and I did so my second year at Mars Hill to get away from the noise and visiting in the dorms.

If a girl wanted to go from her dorm down to the library at night, she must sign out of the dorm, and she had only a set number of minutes to sign in at the library. The process was reversed when she finished her studies at the library.

Needless to say, I never heard of a girl at Mars Hill becoming pregnant and leaving school. No girls going wild at Mars Hill College.

Drinking any alcoholic beverage was prohibited for both boys and girls. One of my friends from North Wilkesboro smuggled in a quart of moonshine. He told us that he sometimes hauled the corn liquor for the moonshiners from the liquor stills to market.

He had a fast car and always drove like he was on a NASCAR track, so this may have been true. We used good judgment and consumed the adult beverage, sometimes called mountain dew or snake bite medicine, off campus and staggered back to the dorms in the wee hours. The significant part of this story is that we didn't get caught.

When I returned to Mars Hill for our fiftieth class reunion, a classmate we will call Ted told me that he had been by Dean Lee's office to "set things straight."

It seems that a house mother reported to Dean Lee that Ted had met, we shall say, "Suzy" down on the bridge below the girls' dorm at 2:00 a.m. Of course, Ted defended Suzy's honor and vigorously denied that this event had occurred.

On Ted's return to Mars Hill for the fifty year reunion, he told us that he had been by Dean Lee's office again and he told Dean Lee that yes, he had, in fact, met Suzy down on the bridge and that he was proud of it.

Of course, Dean Lee had passed on to glory years before, but we can all agree now that Ted was a man of honor who would never betray his lady friend.

Mars Hill girls were not allowed to smoke, but it was okay for boys to smoke. When a Mars Hill coed got the urge to have a smoke, she could always go up to the sandwich shop on Main Street and sit in one of the booths with a boy or two.

If a tattletale came into the establishment (a few souls, and we knew who they were, felt that it was their obligation to report this grave sin to the school authorities), the girls would pass their cigarettes to the boy sitting beside them, and there would be a bunch of Mars Hill guys puffing on cigarettes amply endowed with lipstick. Well, somebody had to do it.

So, did Mars Hill boys really wear lipstick? When the truth is told, maybe not.

43

FOOD FIGHT AT MARS HILL

IT WAS a large room in the basement of what had been a church building. Its first life may have been a place where Sundays schools were held, or where the women of the church held their monthly meetings. It could have been a cold and dreary room, but this was not the case.

The laughter and enthusiasm of underclassmen and pretty wholesome looking coeds of Mars Hill College bounced off of the walls. (They had to be wholesome since Mars Hill's girls were not allowed to smoke, and it goes without saying that there was no imbibing of the spirits of alcohol at this island in the mountains of Western North Carolina.)

This was the happy place that we students at Mars Hill took our meals. We were seated at large wooden tables that sat eight or ten people, and the bowls of food were passed around family style.

Each hungry student took whatever amount that they wanted, and woe be it to those who were seated at a table of football players, for the bowls might be empty before they made the first passing.

I quickly found that seeking out a table with mostly girls was both wise and prudent. The girls were likely to give up their desserts to the guy seated beside them, as well as maybe a carton of milk.

I often took a carton of milk back to Melrose dormitory and placed it in my refrigerator, which was the space between the window and the screen in my room. The cool mountain air would be adequate to refrigerate the milk overnight. These tactics might now be considered as "survival of the fittest."

The food at Mars Hill was tasty and the ladies from the area who did the cooking prepared the food in a similar fashion to my Mother's excellent cooking. We can now pause in reverence and thanks for good ole Southern down-home style cooking.

Speaking of reverence and thanks, it was not unusual for the student seated beside you to bow his or her head in silent prayer before partaking of the food before us. Mars Hill was a school established by the Baptists and there were several students there who planned to become Christian ministers of the gospel. Prayers were not foreign to those who attended Mars Hill in 1949.

Nothing is as constant as change, I suppose, so the administration at Mars Hill decided to build a new dining hall and student center. The student center even had ping pong or table tennis as a feature. There was one student that was exceptionally skillful and everyone tried to beat him, but he always seemed to keep his title as King of the Mountain.

Our food was served cafeteria style at the new dining hall and it was not accepted well by the students, as the quality and the menu was not to their liking. The students rose up in protest and called a meeting that was well attended. It was an orderly meeting, and anyone who wanted to have his or her say could do so.

Mars Hill was a friendly place and everyone smiled and

spoke with one another. Snobs and "stuck up" students did not fit in. The professors led the way and were genuinely concerned with the progress of their students. Still, the campus rules were strictly adhered to.

But food was another matter. The administration listened to our protest and improvements came quickly.

The great food fight at Mars Hill ended with nary a drop of bloodshed, nor were pies smashed in the face of Dean Lee or President Blackwell. They did not resign, and all was well on the hill.

44

FROM MARS HILL TO ALABAMA

MARS HILL COLLEGE had its own unique culture and it evolved around being Baptist. There were a lot of students attending who planned to be Baptist ministers. Their plans were to attend Wake Forest University (another Baptist school) in Winston Salem, as soon as they were graduated from Mars Hill.

Some of these guys lived in my dorm, Melrose. Melrose dormitory was quite austere compared to student lodging today. The bunk beds, a small desk, and a couple of chairs were about all there was.

There was no TV (hadn't been invented yet) or refrigerator to clutter the scene. If you wanted to keep a morsel of food overnight, just raise the window and place the food between the window and the screen. The nights in the Western Carolina Mountains were usually cool enough to do the job.

Of course, there were pre-ministerial students in my classes, in the band, and on the track team. Most of them were pretty regular guys, but there were a few, what I termed "momma's boys," who seemed to live very sheltered lives. *How can they guide their flock through life if they've never lived it?* I often wondered.

I had saved enough money to get me through my first year at Mars Hill with the assistance of ten dollars a month from my rental house, and an occasional gig playing my trombone for a dance with the Teddy Martin Band. But I was going to have to get a job with some fairly decent income during the summer to make up the shortfall for the next year.

Some of the students told me they made a good income selling Bibles and a few other books, door to door, for the Southwestern Bible Company of Nashville. I signed up for the adventure.

And it did become an adventure. I was introduced into a different culture when I was assigned to a territory around Sylacauga, Alabama.

I found that central Alabama was quite different from Western North Carolina. I was made aware of the KKK (Ku Klux Klan) and was warned by my newly acquired Alabama friends not to cross the Klan.

I saw many cotton fields, and I didn't know a cotton-picking thing about cotton (pun intended). I met quite a few Negroes and most were rather shy about talking with this white boy from the mountains, where there were very few black people. (Please note that the term African American was not used in 1951. Black people were called Coloreds or Negroes.)

My father never allowed the "N-word" to be used in our household, but it was quite different in Sylacauga. There were separate bus stops, water fountains and restrooms. Recovery from slavery seemed to be slow a-coming.

Slavery is never a pretty thing, be it the Jews being slaves to the Egyptians, the White Europeans being slaves in the Ottoman Empire, or the Black Africans being slaves in the United States.

It seems that civilization should now be beyond that, but slavery still exists today in many places and forms.

That summer in Alabama plunged me into a different world. Since I was a college student, a couple of girls, who were sisters, that I had met who were also college students, invited me to a party. They were of the elite in the area and they lived in a very large house, almost a mansion.

At this party I met an interesting guy who became an actor and singer named Jim Nabors. He played the role of Gomer Pyle on *The Andy Griffith Show* and was from this section of Alabama.

There was a great deal of attention to what class of society one belonged to in those days. I was accepted for the moment into the upper class in the area, having attended college.

In the fall, I returned to the friendly campus of Mars Hill, where most everyone knew my name...Roy. You see, my name had been placed on the college rolls as Roy Rogers, and when the roll was called in each class as "Roy," I knew who they meant, so I answered loud and clear, "Here!"

Everybody had a good laugh and I was branded as "Roy Rogers." At the time, Roy Rogers was in a lot of cowboy movies and was quite famous. It was all in good fun.

Even today, when I am called Roy Rogers, I answer in jest that Roy is the one who has a horse, and I am the one who has the money. It always gets a good laugh!

45

FROM MELROSE TO MAIN STREET

WHEN I LANDED on the campus of Mars Hill College, both feet were on the ground and I was ready to study and do well. I needed to make up scholastically for not trying very hard to make good grades in Waynesville Township High School. Since I was paying my own way, I wanted to get my money's worth.

I was at the right place. My fellow students were friendly and they spoke to each other in passing. There was not a "stuck up" attitude. It was easy to make friends. There were no fraternity or sorority houses, just the girls' dormitories on one hill and the boys' dorms on another.

I moved into Melrose dorm and was assigned a roommate named George Tanji. He was a small guy with a Japanese father and a Hawaiian mother.

George shivered a lot. He could never acclimate to our cold winters in the mountains. I took George home with me for a weekend and he almost froze in our family's home with no central heat.

Our dorm room was sparse by today's standards, with bunk beds and one small desk. The bathroom was down the hallway and shared with all the other guys on the first floor, but I never heard anyone complain.

My next roommate was Hicks Elmore from Shelby, North Carolina. Hicks was a gregarious guy, and our friends like to congregate in our room to socialize and shoot the bull. Hicks played a pretty hot trumpet in our band, and he liked to talk about what we would do when we went together to the University of North Carolina at Chapel Hill.

But that never happened. I couldn't study with something always going on, so I moved out of the dorm and into a basement room in the home of an older lady who rented out rooms.

The house was nice and was located on Main Street close to campus. It was easy to study there since my roommate was not there much. He was an operator and man about town. If you had a test coming up, he could probably get you a copy. I was never a part of this operation.

Charlie was personally clean, showering every day and wearing nice clothes, but he never washed the sheets until they turned colors. His side of the room was a mess. We had kind of an imaginary line down the center of the room, and I tried to keep a little more order on my side of the room.

I wonder what happened to Charlie. Probably ended up a CEO of some company...

46

THE "M" CLUB

WHEN I ENROLLED at Mars Hill, I never realized I would be so busy. I'd saved enough by working at Ralph's Market for a year and a summer to pay most of my Mars Hill expenses for two years. I didn't have an after school job as I did in high school, so I could enjoy the full college experience.

I did, however, play an occasional gig with The Teddy Martin Band. This was the big band era, so we had fourteen instruments and four vocalists. I played first trombone. It was a lot of fun and I got paid twenty dollars for a gig, which was big money then.

Posters were put up in store windows in the town where the gig was to be played. Teddy had organized a good band, and we always had great attendance at these dances.

We tried to be first class, and wore white dinner jackets with black slacks and bowties. We were a cool bunch sitting behind individual Teddy Martin bandstands.

I joined the Mars Hill marching band and became the drum major. One of our majorettes later became Miss North Carolina, so you can see one reason that I joined the band! But my tenure only lasted through football season, when my interest changed to sports and I joined the cross country Team.

Cross country meets allowed us to travel to other colleges. I enjoyed the travel and the sport, but was not the best on the team. Our star was the smallest guy on the team. He would lay back in the pack most of the race, but near the end he would start moving up and then turn on the steam, usually winning the race.

The coaching budget was meager at Mars Hill, and the assistant football coach had to coach cross country, which he didn't enjoy. The next season, he convinced me to become the cross country coach, an unpaid position. I wouldn't be lying to say that I've coached at a College level—but at best, it's a rather dubious claim.

Since I had boxed a bit in high school, I tried out for the boxing team. A practice match with an upperclassman ended up with him getting a cut over his eye, which he did not take kindly. He was afraid this accidental cut would affect his good looks. This little incident helped me decide to find a better sport, since I didn't want boxing to affect my good looks. (I'm not sure how that worked out.)

This led me to try out for the track team. My best race was the low hurdles and in my second year, and I won all of my races but one. The guy from Davidson University beat me by half a step. But I use this excuse for losing: I had to run on a curved track for the first time. I had previously run on a straight track only. Well, it sounds like a good excuse to me! I also ran on the mile relay team, which did quite well since our kick man (the fastest man) was state champion of South Carolina in high school.

The highlight in my sports career was my picture on the front page of the sports section in the *Asheville Citizen-Times*. I was jumping a hurdle in perfect form. I regret having lost this photo. Oh, well...

The athletes who earned a letter were invited to join the "M" club. The process involved an initiation, which included running through the beltline.

This is the way that it works: The "M" club members took off their belts and stood facing each other in two lines. The new member ran between the lines while the members got to take a swipe with their belts at the victims. Needless to say, the faster you ran, the fewer hits you got. I think I set a speed record going through the beltline.

Some other things done to the new "M" club members were too gross to mention here. But when the process ended, we were awarded a nice sweater and a big "M" letter. We were then bonded forever as an "M" club member.

47

MRS. MCELROY AND "THE GREAT I AM"

AFTER ENROLLING at Mars Hill College and becoming involved in several activities, my mind began to wander back to Hanging Dog. I wasn't really homesick, but I just kept thinking about some of the things that were unique or made me love the place. The little things count more than I realized.

Yes, I missed this spot called Hanging Dog on the outskirts of Waynesville. I remember the cherry trees perched on the hillside above the little shack where I was born. These cherry trees had strong limbs and us kids could climb to our hearts' content and pick copious amounts of this fruit. Mom would make cherry cobblers and even fill fruit jars with a sweet redness to brighten the cold and barren winter months.

I missed seeing the mallard ducks waddle down to the little stream, which we called a branch, then gracefully navigate the water. We needed to regularly patrol the banks to find their eggs, which they seemed to hide from us.

I remembered the rooster crowing, which made an alarm clock unnecessary, I remembered Ole Horney or Buttercup lowing or bawling for no seemingly good reason. They may have just wanted some more hay.

But when their little calves were sold and taken from them, they bawled in protest. They wept for their babies and tried to call them back so they could feed them again. I was sad to hear these barnyard mothers crying out to no avail. But they gave up and stopped after a few days.

But things and animals were not all that I missed. Looking out from the rear of our home across the branch we saw the home of Mrs. McElroy. She frequently would sit on the front porch with Joe Linton, her son. Joe Linton had survived T.B. (tuberculosis), and his sister was confined in a T.B. sanatorium.

The dreaded disease had struck the McElroy family hard, but this was not unusual during the Great Depression. Even today, more people worldwide die of this airborne infectious disease than any other. Since T.B. is almost eradicated in the United States, we don't hear much about it these days. It is curable now, but wasn't back when the McElroys had it.

Mrs. McElroy's white clapboard house was small but neat and well kept. The pump organ in the living room was an indication of better times in her household. My sister Jane saw the organ and asked Mrs. McElroy if she should play it. When mother learned that Jane had entered the house to play the organ, she warned Jane not to do it again. Mother feared there may have still been T.B. germs lurking there.

If someone would make an unusual remark, Mrs. McElroy would raise her hands in the air and proclaim "The Great I Am." Us kids never knew what she meant.

Actually, she was praising the greatness of God as mentioned in Exodus 3:13-14 and other places in the Bible where God is referred to as "I Am."

Mrs. McElroy and Joe Linton sat on their little porch and

listened to the gurgling of the stream flowing by their house. They never complained. They smiled and talked with all who passed by, even the children.

PART VIII

RATH

48
———

WHO THREW THAT HAM AT ME?

Mornings came early in Waterloo, Iowa. The Baby Ben alarm clock went off at 5:00 a.m., and five student salesmen of Rath Packing Company made quick use of the one bathroom on the second floor of the home of the elderly couple who rented rooms to them. No lingering allowed!

No appliances for preparing food came with my room. There was no refrigerator and no oven. We took all of our meals out, so the hungry five piled into the 1939 Ford owned by the oldest member of our group and we headed toward the plant cafeteria provided by Rath for the employees.

There were fried potatoes in ample supply along with Rath's smoked sausages, and of course there were scrambled eggs. This boy from the mountains of Western North Carolina had never eaten potatoes for breakfast before, but they were well prepared and perfect for stoking the engines of the men and women who did the hard work at the packing house.

Rath Packing Company, which made Black Hawk bacon famous, probably had the best training program in the industry for their salesmen. The sales training director was more like a college professor, and his classes were well organized and thorough.

One class member from New York City asked what was the difference between a pig and a hog. This brought laughter from the class, and later we had to explain to him the difference between a steer and a bull. This difference is determined by the absence or presence of what we called mountain oysters.

(I'm being as delicate as I can with this subject. Another difference is that bull meat is tough and steer meat is more tender.)

Our training was not only in the classroom, but we got to work a week or two in each major department of the world's largest packing plant on one site. The plant was six stories high and covered acres. You could get lost going from one department to another.

It was hands-on training, and watching a muscular man with a sledgehammer crack the skull of a bovine with one well-placed blow was not for the faint of heart. The animals fell to the floor immediately and they never knew what hit them. This was cruelty in its most humane form at the time.

The men who swung the hammers and looked into the eyes of these animals seldom lasted very long on this job. I think this killing of innocent animals eventually tore at their souls, but this was the price paid for a good steak or hamburger.

The processing of lamb had a bizarre twist. Today, when we go to a fine restaurant and order lamb chops or roast leg of lamb, this is the end of a process. The process starts when a truckload of lambs are delivered to the packing house and placed in holding pens. The lambs then must be delivered to the killing floor in an orderly manner.

It is difficult to drive sheep, but they will willingly follow a goat. This job fell to Judas. Judas was a goat who received his name from the Bible story where Jesus was betrayed by Judas for thirty pieces of silver.

Judas the goat would go down to the pen of lambs and the innocent lambs would follow Judas back to the killing floor, a dastardly act of betrayal. Judas would be rewarded, not with thirty pieces of silver, but with a cigarette. He liked cigarettes but he never smoked them, preferring to chew them instead.

Most of the men and women at the plant were well fed—not obese, but able to handle their challenging jobs. However, there was one outstanding young lady who worked on the production line that disassembled a hog. She would have been able, with her assets, to be a Playboy centerfold.

The workers on this production line had to periodically sharpen their knives. When this sweet young thang started this sharpening process, it set in motion her ample assets. This did not go unnoticed by the red-blooded men on the line, and in unison they would bang their knives on the metal work tables in front of them as they roared their appreciation. Comic relief was possible in the most mundane of occupations.

Some departments were highly unionized, and others not so much. A department that was mostly union would quickly show us what they did and then suggest that we go to the locker room and play cards or catch up on our sleep. There really was not enough work to go around and they didn't want this to be evident. I soon decided that I would rather work than be a slug in the locker room.

Union led strikes could be serious business, and the company placed men with rifles on roofs above the picket lines. It was a brave man indeed who would attempt to cross these picket lines, manned by brawny men and women who were not afraid to back up their words. When we became salesmen out in the field, we usually got raises after a strike, even though we were non-union.

In the beef grading department, an older gentleman taught me how to grade beef and determine if it was U.S. Prime, Choice, Good, Commercial...or Utility (ugh!). This gentleman had an extra ticket to the University of Iowa football games that he sometimes let me use. We would stop at one of the Amish restaurants for some excellent food on our way back to Waterloo.

A lot of the employees worked in coolers that were quite frosty, and they dressed in layers of warm clothing. There were security men at the exits, but this didn't deter some hardy souls from bootlegging some choice products past security under their bulky coats.

One man was exiting the premises with a ham concealed under his coat, and just as he passed security, the ham slipped and bounced off his foot. This quick-thinking man immediately jumped back and yelled, "Who threw that ham at me?" More comic relief at the Rath Packing Company.

49

THE BULLY ON BROAD STREET

WHEN I WAS a young salesman for Rath Packing Company, one of my duties was to call on retail stores, small packing houses and other distributors of meat-related products. In order to make sales, good customer relations had to be established.

When I took over the sales territory of Augusta, Georgia, one of my customers was on a C.O.D. (Cash On Delivery) basis due to his past experience with Rath. His little "supermarket" was located on Broad Street, the main street of Augusta. One day he approached me and asked if his account could be taken off C.O.D. terms. I processed his request, and on my recommendation Rath established an open account arrangement. He seemed grateful, and his meat market manager increased the size of his orders with Rath.

When I telegraphed my coded orders daily to the packing house in Waterloo, the meat products were loaded into a refrigerated eighteen-wheeler and, on arrival in Augusta, the products were sorted on a large loading platform and delivered to my customers by smaller delivery trucks under contract with Rath.

I received a call from my delivery vendor that this customer, who I will refer to as Bubba, had refused delivery of the rather large order his market manager had given me. The product had been placed in the vendor's cooler until I could resell the items. This would be at a substantial discount, or loss.

I went by to see Bubba and asked if something was wrong with the order. If so, we would try to make it right.

"If you don't like it, we will just go outside and settle it," Bubba replied.

"I didn't come here to fight, Bubba. I just wanted to know if something was wrong."

But he simply repeated his invitation.

Here was the situation: I was a tall, skinny guy who wore glasses. Bubba, I'd been told, was a semi-pro boxer and was bigger than me. I wasn't going to run, so I had no option but to walk outside thinking I was probably in for a royal ass-whupping.

"Take off those G—D— glasses," Bubba barked, as we stepped onto the sidewalk in front of the store.

I obliged, and immediately he threw a haymaker at me.

A haymaker is a long looping kind of blow usually aimed at the head and meant to be a knockout punch. He didn't know that I'd boxed a little in high school and in college. So instead of falling away from his haymaker as a non-boxer would have done, I stepped inside of the haymaker as my boxing instincts took over.

My left arm went around his head, and with all my adrenaline pumping, I pummeled his face like a jackhammer with my right fist. I virtually demolished his face in a few seconds. He grabbed me around the waist and we both hit the sidewalk.

Here comes the ass-whupping, I thought, as he and I got up. But to my surprise, he just walked back into the store. He had had enough. If Bubba was surprised not to have flattened the skinny meat salesman, he wasn't half as surprised as I was.

I hustled back to my apartment before anyone could call the police, and put a band-aid or two on my skinned knee, my only injury. I thanked the Lord that he had taken care of me. Then I went back to my sales route, not knowing what to expect next.

As it turns out, in the meat business, there is a well-oiled communication network. When I called on my customers later, they already knew about the street fight—and were smiling about the outcome.

A few doors down Broad Street from Bubba's place was another little "supermarket" owned by an older gentleman named Mr. Anderson. A couple of days after the fight, I called on Mr. Anderson. He actually hugged me and doubled my order in gratitude. On the way to see Mr. Anderson, I walked by Bubba's store, and as I glanced into the store I saw Bubba standing by a vegetable stand with a still-swollen face. There is a God.

The next week, my sales manager notified that he would be going with me on my sales route, and told me to pick him up at a hotel on Broad Street. I pulled my company car, with Chief Black Hawk's image on the doors, to the curb and told my manager there was something he needed to know.

I thought he would probably fire me when he learned that his salesman was a street fighter, but he only grinned. Looks like someone had filled him in—you know how that meat business network works—but maybe he had noticed how most of my orders were larger than before.

Thanks again, Bubba, for giving my business a shot in the arm.

50

VANITY RULES

I TRIED to unlock the door to the 1939 black Ford, but the key didn't seem to fit.

There were probably millions of black Ford out there on America's streets. Henry Ford, who pioneered the assembly line concept to produce automobiles the common man could afford, also offered another cost-cutter. You could get a T-model Ford in black...or black. Multiple color options would increase the cost of the car.

"Give me the damn key, if you can't even open a car door! You must be drunk," said Mighty Mike.

Mighty Mike came from New York City—and it was written all over him. He gave it a try or two without any success and with a big sign of disgust muttered, "Hell, I must be drunk too."

The key just would not fit, and we were giving up trying to unlock the black Ford when we noticed a baby bed in the back seat of the car.

"Do you normally carry a baby bed in your car?" Mike asked.

We looked down the street and there it was, another black

1939 Ford. The key fit and I was not too inebriated to negotiate a path back to our place of residence without incident.

Mike and I were fellow Sales Trainees at Rath in Waterloo. We'd decided that a night on the town would relieve the stresses of our meager existence. We found a nightclub with entertainment provided, without a cover charge, which we could not afford.

The entertainer was an organist who was dressed in garments that were frilly and feminine. The entertainer started flirting with Mike and he returned the favor, so guess who visited our table at break time? The entertainer, who happened to be a female impersonator.

Needless to say, Mighty Mike was madder than wildcat in a tow sack when he discovered his little error in identity, and he was not reluctant to let me know how he felt about me not letting him know that his dream girl was a man.

You see, Mike was rather vain regarding wearing his glasses. So I, with aid of my eyepieces could detect the nature of the beast, whereas Mike did not know who he was flirting with.

"Why in the hell didn't you tell me?" he said to me.

My answer to Mighty Mike from New York City was simple.

"Next time, Michael, you will wear your damn glasses."

But I don't remember there being a next time.

51

THE FBI COMES KNOCKING

IT WAS early morning and I was preparing to go to work, picking out the tie I would wear that day. As a young salesman for Rath Packing Company in 1953, I was required to wear a coat and tie.

I was surprised by a knock on the door. Who would come calling so early? Maybe it was my sweet landlady, who rented me the garage apartment behind her large two-story frame house. I was lucky to find this little place to call home located on "The Hill" section of Augusta, which was the more desirable part of town.

I answered the door and was faced with two gentlemen dressed in dark-colored suits. They flipped open their leather wallets to show their identity.

"We're with the FBI, could we come in and talk with you?" they asked politely.

My mind raced back to what was an adventure for me. My new bride and I had borrowed my Dad's car to drive to Monterrey, Mexico. I couldn't drive my company car, and besides, it had the Rath Packing Company logo on both front doors: the image of Chief Black Hawk in full headdress.

My Dad had been generous to allow me the use of his only vehicle, but he was a kind and generous man. Could some drug dealer somehow have put some drugs in the structure of Dad's auto?

In driving across some semi-desert landscape in Mexico, we had a flat tire, and when I installed the spare I found it was low on air. We limped into the next town, which consisted of a service station, a cantina and a few goats wandering about.

Two men repaired the tires using the basic tools that I had seen in my childhood, when people had lots of flat tires and tires were lined with rubber tubes. Changing flat tires was a frequent occurrence in those days. After much hammering and banging around, the men pumped air into the tires via a hand-operated pump. They had no air gauge and I was trying to stop them, with my limited Spanish, from overinflating my tires. I am sure they must have thought, "gringo loco."

We drove on without incident into Monterrey, Mexico. This was our first visit to a foreign country, and I had never witnessed such poverty, even though I grew up seeing a lot of neighbors and family in Hanging Dog doing without.

There were unattended children all about, some sleeping in doorways of businesses at night. How could this be? If you parked your car on the street, a swarm of little boys would suddenly appear who volunteered to "watch your car" and prevent damage while you were away. I always kept plenty of pesos and tried to give every one of them their share to keep Dad's car safe.

Could an older brother of these little guys put the drugs in the car? I had read of this happening.

These children of the streets were quite innovative in finding ways to obtain a few extra pesos. Some would say "I can take you to my sister, she is very beautiful." A few pesos could stop the hunger pains...there was no obesity with these barefoot children. There was sadness in my heart as we walked from our hotel to a fine restaurant nearby and saw the children still on the streets as the night was falling.

I invited the FBI men into my apartment not knowing what would transpire. I knew that the FBI was at the top of the food chain in law enforcement, so this must be important.

"Do you have a scar on the instep of your left foot?" one of them asked me.

I took off my shoe and there it was, plain as day, a long forgotten scar from my carefree, barefoot childhood.

I could almost hear them thinking, *We have our man.*

"Do you have a scar on your upper back?" was the next question.

As I removed my shirt for their inspection, I was wondering the same thing. *Do I possibly have a scar, long forgotten, on my back?*

Boy, was I relieved when they found no such scar. No trip downtown in handcuffs in the back seat of a black FBI sedan!

After a few more questions, they told me that they were looking for an army deserter named Johnny Mack. I happened to know Johnny Mack, who had a lot of physical similarities to me. Like me, he was also from Haywood County.

After some thought, I figured out how they must have gotten my name and address. I'd sent a Christmas card to one of my aunts, and the FBI was apparently checking her mail. You see, Johnny Mack was also a nephew of this aunt from the other side of my family.

The lesson to be learned from this story is that one should never send a Christmas card to an aunt! Otherwise, you might get a knock on the door and the question, "We are with the FBI, could we come in and talk with you?"

ACKNOWLEDGMENTS

I'd like to thank Kim Frazier, who took my first drafts, written on a legal pad, and changed them to typewritten form, even correcting my spelling.

Thanks to JoAnna Bridges and Santana Fitzpatrick at The Claiborne for scanning my handwritten drafts and getting them to my son Bradford.

Also, thanks to Carolyn at Book Mart in Starkville, MS, for setting up signings there, introducing me to other authors, and generally looking out for me.

A special shout out to those who attended my October 2018 book signing at Book Mart: Lucy, Derrick, Jeannie, Johnny Wayne and Nancie Bradford, Dick and Nancy Juge, Mary Todd and Foster, Christina, Charlene, Billy, Melba Rose, Danny Paul, Leah, Brenda, Theresa, Hunter, Norma, Marie, Mary Ann, Adelaide, Jerry and Tommy.

Special thanks go to Mary Todd (and Foster), our Sidewalk Outreach Crew.

And finally, this book would not have been possible without

the help of my editor (and son) Bradford Rogers—who I'm sure, as the editor, would not have inserted himself here in the Acknowledgements section. ;-)

ALSO BY RAY B. ROGERS

Depression Baby

*Get the audiobook free, along with a free month of Audible, the
world's premier audiobook publisher.*

ABOUT THE AUTHOR

Ray B. Rogers grew up in Western North Carolina, attended Mars Hill College; and graduated from the University of NC at Chapel Hill with a B.S. in Business Administration.

Ray is married to Lucy Rogers and lives in Starkville and Louisville, Mississippi. He has two sons, Bradford Rogers and Derrick Goldben.

For over 57 years, Ray owned a State Farm Insurance Agency and was National President of the State Farm Agents Association.

 facebook.com/RayBRogers

twitter.com/RayBRogers

instagram.com/RayBRogers

58860224R00117

Made in the USA
Columbia, SC
26 May 2019